INFINITE
WORDS

ALSO BY ZANE

Addicted
Shame on It All
The Heat Seekers
The Sex Chronicles: Shattering the Myth
Gettin' Buck Wild: The Sex Chronicles II
The Sisters of APF
Nervous
Skyscraper
Afterburn
Love is Never Painless
Dear G-Spot: Straight Talk About Sex and Love
Zane's The Sex Chronicles
Total Eclipse of the Heart
The Hot Box
Everything Fades Away
I'll Be Home for Christmas
The Other Side of the Pillow

EDITED BY ZANE

Chocolate Flava
Caramel Flava
Succulent: Chocolate Flava II
Honey Flava
Sensuality: Caramel Flava II
Z-Rated: Chocolate Flava III
Busy Bodies: Chocolate Flava IV
Breaking the Cycle
Purple Panties
Missionary No More: Purple Panties 2
Blackgentlemen.com
Sistergirls.com
Another Time, Another Place

INFINITE WORDS

A COMPREHENSIVE GUIDE TO WRITING AND PUBLISHING

Zane

ATRIA PAPERBACK

NEW YORK   LONDON   TORONTO   SYDNEY   NEW DELHI

ATRIA PAPERBACK
An Imprint of Simon & Schuster, Inc.
1230 Avenue of the Americas
New York, NY 10020

First Atria Paperback edition March 2015

ATRIA PAPERBACK and colophon are trademarks of Simon & Schuster, Inc.

For information about special discounts for bulk purchases, please contact Simon & Schuster Special Sales at 1-866-506-1949 or business@simonandschuster.com.

The Simon & Schuster Speakers Bureau can bring authors to your live event. For more information or to book an event, contact the Simon & Schuster Speakers Bureau at 1-866-248-3049 or visit our website at www.simonspeakers.com.

Interior design by Kyoko Watanabe
Cover design by Janet Perr
Cover photographs and lettering © Shutterstock

Manufactured in the United States of America

10 9 8 7 6 5 4 3 2 1

Library of Congress Cataloging-in-Publication Data is available.

ISBN 978-1-4767-6696-6
ISBN 978-1-4767-6697-3 (ebook)

Contents

✳

Contents

Part 2

PUBLISHING

117

Part 3

WRITING EXERCISES

189

Introduction

*

After seventeen years in the publishing business, I decided that it was time to finally pen this book, a comprehensive guide to writing and publishing. While the novice writer can benefit from this book, I am especially writing this for those people who have a desire to establish long-lasting careers in the industry.

Writing one book is rather simplistic; the question of success or failure aside, you set out to accomplish that goal, complete it, and let the chips fall where they may. A lot of people only want to write one book, particularly those who want to pen a memoir or a self-help book based on their own experiences, or those who want to get one major point across—and there is nothing wrong with that. Others want to write a book to make some fast money. *Everything* is wrong with that. Does it mean that that concept can never, ever work? No. It means the odds of it happening are very rare.

I was having a conversation recently about the number of authors who disappear from the scene every single year. A lot of that is a consequence of their initial purpose for writing. If your motivation is money, you won't likely succeed. What drives you to do the work of writing a book should be based in sincerity and passion, otherwise a lasting career is nearly impossible or, at best, unlikely.

My passion for books started at a very young age, probably around two or three, when I first started reading. Once I entered middle school, you would never catch me without a book either in my hands or nearby. I was born with a vivid imagination, and my mind never shuts down. I confirmed that recently when I participated in a sleep study and they showed me a printout of my dreams. I dream four times more than the average person throughout the night. Even when my physical body is exhausted, my brain is on overdrive. Becoming a writer as an adult was a natural progression from who I was as a child. All of my teachers prophesied it as I went through school, and it turns out that they were right. At this point, I cannot even imagine doing anything else as a career. I am blessed to never feel like I am actually working.

This book is for published and unpublished authors alike who want to achieve that same feeling. After all, the biggest room in anyone's house is the room for improvement. Too many people reach a certain point and fail to realize that they can go even further beyond the sight line. A true writer always craves to become better and better. A true writer wants to be challenged, even if they create those challenges themselves. Writing is an amazing concept, whether it is done as a hobby, professionally, or simply to vent. Continual evolution is a part of life, whether we want to embrace it or reject it.

Not everyone who thinks they want to will be able to write a book or become a published author. Many will have to settle for finding other outlets for their emotions, like art or music. The process of writing does not fit every person's temperament, and a creative spirit does not have to be confined to one medium. Writing professionally may not be your strong point, but do not give it up. Find other ways to express yourself, and continue to write for your own personal benefit. Writing is a process which can help you express yourself in other areas of your life and can be both healing and cleansing.

In this book I cover all of the elements needed to create what I call "the perfect storm" of creative writing. Stirring up this perfect storm requires learning what it takes to create, be compassionate, and transform and revolutionize lives all at the same time. That has always been my purpose in writing. Even now, with this book about the book industry, it is still my imperative to accomplish those three things.

Part 1 of the book is about writing, while Part 2 is concerned with the steps of publishing. I provide you with writing samples and exercises in Part 3.

There are keys to success and there are keys to failure. I delve into both within these pages. I tell you what to do to flourish and how to prevent withering away. So if you are ready to embark on this road together, let us begin.

PART 1

WRITING AND THE CREATIVE PROCESS

CHAPTER 1

Discipline

Forming Your Writing Habits

Finding the time to write can be a major factor in the lives of most aspiring writers with other careers and responsibilities. Even for those of us who are full-time, successful writers, it can still be a painstaking chore to lock ourselves away with a pen, pad, or a laptop to embrace our passion. I say *passion* because it goes hand in hand with discipline. It comes down to how bad you want to be able to complete a manuscript. While there is no surefire method to the madness that brings about much reward, I have a few suggestions.

First and foremost, do not panic over it. That will solve nothing and will only set you back in your efforts. Even if you have a book under contract and the publisher has established a deadline, you should not feel compelled to turn in something that is not what you consider your best effort. Speak up in the beginning if you do not feel like you can make an established deadline. The publisher can push the date back or, if there is space in the timeline, allow you some extra time.

I am also a publisher, and here's an example: this morning an agent called me and asked if her author could turn in her manuscript in February of next year instead of November of this year. I agreed immediately and amended the paperwork. I do not want my authors to feel like turning in a rough draft is acceptable. I will discuss that in more depth in another chapter. Stressing yourself out is the least effective way to complete a well-written book.

Secondly, be realistic about how often you can write and your writing speed. Some people write a page a day. Others write ten thousand words a day. Most writers fall somewhere in between—*anywhere* in between. Then there are those that may write for a couple of weeks, take a couple of months or even a couple of years off, and then write for another couple of weeks. It all depends.

However, I am an avid believer that if you want to truly be a writer, you will do it daily so that it becomes routine, like brushing your teeth. Even if you have writer's block, it is imperative that you keep the habit up. Write about another topic instead of the one you are stuck on—whatever comes to mind. If you keep it real with yourself about your abilities, then all the pressure floats away.

Thirdly, you need to test different places and times of day to see when you are most effective. Some people write better in the middle of an Internet café, Starbucks, or the dining section of their local grocery store. They like background noise and are inspired by observing people going about their day. Others still feel the power in numbers but noise irritates them, so they may write in the quiet room of the local library. Then there are "the loners." The writers that prefer total isolation so they can immerse themselves in their imaginations. They may have some background noise like the television or listen to some music. Some even have particular songs that motivate them to keep going. I have done all of the above at one time or another. My needs vary so I mix it up. However, if I had to pick one way to write, it would be with music. I have written some books and listened to the same "theme song" practically the entire time that it took to complete them. You need to experiment with different things and see what works best for you.

The biggest key to discipline as a writer is time management. You can find the opportunity to do it by tweaking some of the other things you waste time on. When I first started writing, I was working a full-time, stressful career. However, I made the commitment to spend at least four hours per day working on my passion after spending eight to ten hours a day working on someone else's passion. Instead of hanging out at happy hours after work with co-workers, watching television for several hours, or talking on the phone, I entertained myself with my mind. And the funny part is that when I was doing it from 1997 to 1999, the thought never crossed my mind about actually publishing anything. I would have continued writing, even if that decision was never made.

Also, writing comes easier with a clear head. I would suggest working out—even if it's just walking—prior to writing, or possibly going for a drive, doing a jigsaw puzzle, logic puzzles, or even washing dishes. Whatever works for you personally. Journaling is a great thing as well. Writing down all of your personal concerns in a journal and then leaving it all there frees you up to explore something better or more interesting. There is a great free website called penzu.com that will provide you with a password-protected journal that you can access from anywhere. A lot of people are apprehensive about keeping a hard copy journal because their privacy can be so easily violated. I have had that experience and it was not pleasant. However, the beauty of journaling is that you can go back years, even decades later, and witness where you were in that space and time. Sometimes it renews your beliefs and reminds you how special you are. Other times it shows you how far you have come and how much you have matured. And yes, there are those times when you read your old journals and wonder what the hell you were thinking. Memories are all valuable, positive or negative. The site will even send you a daily reminder email that it is time to write and you can take that as your cue to journal or work on your book. Even if you do not do that, set an alarm to go off on your cell phone to let you know when it is writing time.

Always have something handy to write with, whether it is a tablet, phone, pen and pad, or computer. Even the most prolific writers come up with incredible ideas and then cannot remember them later if they do not write them down. I am still trying to remember what I considered to be the perfect book title a couple of years later. I hope it comes back to me one day because I regret not writing it down. You will have to learn how to zone the rest of the world out when necessary. In today's society, there are even more distractions than there were a decade ago. But I contend that if you want something bad enough, you will do whatever it takes, even if you have to think outside of the box. Most people do not have endless leisure time because of work and family responsibilities, but you will have to hold yourself accountable to make the time to write. Like all habits—bad or good—once you establish one it is easier to keep going and harder to break it.

Developing a Mind-set

When I first began to write, it was not with the intention of becoming published. It was a creative outlet for me. I gave away my musings for free over the Internet for more than three years. Other people began to enjoy my work, but if no one ever had, I still would have continued to write and share. I've now written and published more books than I can count, but truth be told, the majority of the things that I have written still remain unpublished and might very well stay that way. Some are incomplete novels, others are short stories in which I was simply venting about something bothering me. A lot of the writing I've done is in the form of personal journal entries about my life. So not everything I write will have its moment in the sun.

This is the same for most writers. I've read thousands of books, manuscripts, and screenplays in my role as publisher and acquiring editor for my imprint, Strebor Books. Unlike a lot of authors who are constantly in full battle gear and act like we are all gladiators in an arena, I thrive from helping other writers achieve their goals. Can I help everyone? No. Do I even care to help everyone? No.

My decision to publish, mentor, or assist someone is based on many factors. The most important one is whether or not I sense they are serious about writing. Then I have to believe that they are compassionate toward the plight of others. Is that a requirement to be a good writer? Possibly not, but I believe that it is. Unless you can feel empathy, I am not sure how you can create characters whom others will identify with. Even if you are writing a nonfiction book, you still should possess that trait.

Passion is essential as well. If the passion doesn't exist, a writer will quickly fizzle out and tap out of the fight before even putting forth any real effort. They will find a way to shift the blame on others for their own lack of accomplishments and perhaps exhibit a sense of entitlement as they pursue help from others to achieve their goals. A few people email me with that attitude. They are not concerned with my workload, my family and responsibilities; they expect everything to revolve around them, and they do not even know me. All of this, and when I finally extend the olive branch, they inform me that they have not actually completed a book.

If you are meant to be published, it will happen eventually. You have to have the patience to submit your book to existing publishers and work with their schedules and timing, or you can self-publish on your own time and terms. That is the fastest way to get a book out and see what happens, but if you go that route, please make sure that your work is properly edited and packaged well. I offer information and advice in this book on how to self-publish as well.

Once you've completed a manuscript and are seeking a deal, or pursuing the self-publishing route, continue to write other things. Experiment with different techniques and in different genres; push yourself to the limit. Observe the world around you and then go home and make up a short story about someone you saw out and about that day. Let your imagination run rampant. Exercise your brain.

CHAPTER 2

Writing Style– Only You Can Define It

What Makes Someone a Writer?

If you have ever written something down that you needed to get off of your chest because your brain felt like it was overloaded, you are a writer. It may have been a poem, a short story, an entire manuscript, or even a simple quote that you made up. It is all writing, but you must define your writing style and that is based on your overall purpose and vision. The most important thing is to take your time because rushing takes away from the experience for most.

Cultivating a Writing Style

Your writing style is the way that you choose to present your concepts and thoughts to a potential reading audience. There are many writing elements that contribute to creating a perfect storm. They include grammar, diction, clichés, punctuation, connotation, dialogue, situation, and purpose. They will all vary based on the premise of the book. For example, if you are writing a young adult novel, the diction and dialogue should be indicative of how teenagers speak and connect with one another. Then you have to break that down further, based on the region of the country where the story takes place, the characters' educational background, and their overall living conditions and influences. Now, if it is a historical novel, everything changes and you need to do research to make sure all of the elements are as authentic as possible. Readers will pick up on things that do not mesh correctly; that is for sure.

PIE

The first thing you need to determine is how you can make a PIE (Persuade, Inform, and Entertain) without losing the attention span of readers or confusing them to the point of no return. One of my many roles for the past seventeen years has been as a life coach/advice columnist. When I post certain advice emails on Facebook, there are often dozens of comments from readers who need clarification on what the person who emailed me is attempting to say. Now, they are not professional writers and I often rephrase it when I realize it will be a major issue. My point is that a lot of people have not been taught the proper way to communicate their ideas. It will likely get worse as society turns more toward text messages, emails, and social networking to communicate instead of actual speaking. Soon we will be faced with a generation of young adults who can barely hold a conversation with one another in person. It is a truly sad plight that is quickly coming to pass. A good writer is a good communicator—both on and off the page. They can make PIEs with their books and they can make PIEs when they speak in person.

Learn to Write by Reading

Read as many books as you can. One of the silliest statements that I have ever heard is a writer saying that they do not read because they do not want another writer's work to influence their own. That is absurd! I read every single day, publish between thirty-six and sixty books a year, and never once have I ever had a fleeting thought about using someone else's ideas. I became a writer because I loved and appreciated reading. From a very early age, my parents instilled a love of reading in me. In the third grade, my mother enrolled me in a speed-reading class and, by the sixth grade, I was reading a book a day. I feel naked and depressed without something to read when the urge hits me. It is nearly impossible to become a great writer without reading great books. That is not to say that you need to copy someone else's techniques, but you need to recognize good technique. Too many people feel like they can simply throw a book together and the world will not be able to recognize exactly what they did.

There are mediocre books that have become commercially successful with the right marketing and support. I have seen it happen. In fact, I recently decided against publishing a book that I immediately assumed had to be great based on self-published sales. I was ready to make a two-book offer but then decided to set aside a day and actually read it. I was honest with the author. I told him I thought the work was poorly written and wished him well. He was talking about putting out two more books later on in the same year, and I suggested that he study the craft of writing a little bit more. As a traditional publisher, I realized that all professional reviews would be negative and that his book, which was selling for ninety-nine cents, could not sell nearly as many copies at even ten dollars and less at fifteen.

Whether fiction or nonfiction, you should attempt to persuade readers to think something that they may not normally lean toward thinking. You may be trying to persuade them to do something major like recommitting their life to Christ, or something more inane like running through freshly fallen snow barefoot. You could be trying to convince them that you can be successful in life despite having to overcome incredible odds, or that single mothers can do as good of a job raising boys as men can.

You should attempt to inform them of something that they never knew. It could be something heavy and historical (e.g. prior to becoming president, John Adams defended the eight British soldiers who had fired upon citizens during the Boston Massacre) or something humorous and inconsequential (e.g. owls are the only species of birds that can see the color blue). Lastly, and often most importantly, the readers should feel entertained. Books are competing with a dozen-plus other media, not to mention platforms like the iPad and Xbox, after all. You have to cause them to feel something—to laugh, cry, get angry, feel sympathy.

SWOT: Strengths, Weaknesses, Opportunities, Threats

On your pathway to becoming a published author, I would like to suggest that you do a SWOT analysis every three to six months. It is a simple process where you take about an hour to write down four lists: your strengths, your weaknesses, your opportunities, and your threats. What are your overall strengths when it comes to writing? Your overall weaknesses? Are you better at writing narrative than dialogue, or vice versa? Do you write stronger in first person or third person? Are you good at outlining your story or does it traumatize you to even think about it? Determine your strong points and weak points and make a concerted effort to improve on them both.

Strategies for Improvement, or How to Grow Yourself as a Writer

When it comes to opportunities, are there any that exist in the literary world for you? Is there a local writers group you can join? Do you have any friends with connections? Do you live in an area where there are a lot of literary events you can attend? Are there any competitions you can enter to try to get exposure for your work? Is there a published author willing to mentor you who actually has the time to do it? As for threats, you need to list everything that is preventing you from achieving your dream, from dream stealers and reality stealers masked as your friends and relatives to yourself, if you allow laziness and self-doubt to prevent you from writing on a regular basis.

Do not fret if your initial SWOT analysis is terrifying. That is the entire purpose of the exercise: to lay all of your proverbial cards on the table. The objective is to be able to become aware of and completely remove some threats three to six months down the road, add to the list of opportunities, and move some of your weaknesses to your strengths list. You cannot get to where you want to be without understanding where you currently are. That applies to every aspect of life, and you can use this same analysis for an overall self-assessment. I even do one with my college-aged daughter at least twice a year. It is a marvelous tool and it costs nothing but a few moments of your time. It yields greatly beneficial information that you may not even recognize about yourself until you see it on paper in black and white.

Six Basic Human Needs

Successful writing is highly dependent on the ability to touch upon what many call "the six basic human needs." They are, in no particular order: certainty, uncertainty, connection, contribution, significance, and growth.

If you have ever wondered why social networking is so powerful, one of the main reasons is because people experience the full range of these emotions on the most popular sites. They feel connected to those they know, as well as complete strangers. They feel significant because they can announce that they cooked chicken and rice for dinner and people will like their post. They experience constant growth based on the number of friends or followers they obtain. They feel like they are contributing to something by reposting or sharing what someone else says, or by commenting on a discussion thread. They have a sense of certainty because they know that they can log on anytime, day or night, and the service will be there. They feel a sense of uncertainty from reading about negative news—which always seems to spread like wildfire, while positive items seem to quickly disappear from one's newsfeed.

When you are writing, you need to focus on stimulating intelligence, pulling at the heartstrings, and inciting both hope and fear in your readers. A good book may not be popular at the time it is initially published but can nonetheless come to be regarded as a classic over time. And a film can be wildly popular at the time it is released but soon forgotten. Every year, studios make movies that make a ton of money at the box office, but less than two months later no one is even discussing them. They were entertaining but did not have a long-lasting impact. Then there are movies, often made on a lower budget or independently, that are so persuasive, informative, and entertaining that people watch them two or three generations later. Case in point, how many holiday seasons in a row has *It's a Wonderful Life* been played on television consecutively? For decades, right? That is because the premise of the story transcends time, and it is still touching and memorable long after the original 1946 release date. Nearly seven decades have passed and people still appreciate it, cry over it, and embrace it, even if they watch it every single time it comes on. That is one hell of a PIE!

I will give you another analogy. There is a yearly women's conference held in Anyplace, USA. More than two thousand women from all over the globe attend to be uplifted, empowered, and motivated. It is a three-day conference and there is a powerful lineup of speakers, one per day. So on the first day, the one we will call Rebecca takes the stage. Her reputation precedes her since she is the top CEO in her industry. She gives an amazing speech that results in a standing ovation. As the women leave the ballroom, they discuss the speech, but by the time dinnertime rolls around the discussion has pretty much died down.

The next day, the one we will call Trish takes the stage. She is another top-notch CEO, makes a couple million per year, and looks every bit the part. She gives yet another amazing speech and gets a standing ovation as well. The women are still discussing what was said over dinner that night and into the next morning. A few of them will go back home and share key points with their friends and relatives, but the fascination will wear off within a month's time.

On closing day, the one we will call Lisa walks up on stage. Like her counterparts, she has made a name for herself in corporate America and is wealthy, successful, and on track to cash out upon retirement with tens of millions in bonuses. Her speech is life-changing. Not only does she get a standing ovation but many of the women are in tears, some are clinging to each other like they're experiencing a spiritual revival, and others remain seated, simply dumbfounded and speechless, completely taken off guard because they have been so moved. They leave the convention in Anyplace, USA, prepared to overcome any obstacle, any setback, any drama, any financial issues, any family issues, and everything in between to get where they desire to be.

A good book inspires people. A good book causes an

impact. A good book sparks thought, motivates, frightens, uplifts, angers—sometimes all of those things at once—but it begins with you defining your purpose for writing.

Now everything that I wrote in this chapter is going to go completely over the heads of anyone who wants to write a book simply to say that they wrote a book. People that are only interested in writing because they think they can make a lot of money will not care about any of my advice. They will continue to throw something together and believe that they are on the top of the writing craft because their limited fan base tells them so. They will put something out on the market or turn it in to their publisher without even doing a single read-through of it. While they may obtain some limited success, the writing community as a whole will never respect them.

There are many authors who have been published for a long time but have not been able to increase their readership base. One of the main reasons is because they have become too formulaic. They stifle their ability to gain more readers by writing with the same tone and the same overall premise over and over again. They cannot connect to more readers unless they expand their own views and writing topics. That does not mean that they have to change their genre, but they certainly need to attempt to improve upon that genre with each and every book that they offer to the public. Even when you look at popular movie franchises or television shows, they run their courses after a while. No matter how successful a writer becomes, they have to change things up from time to time. Don't believe me? Take a good look at some of the top authors in the game and see how they have done that very thing.

You need a lot of patience in this business. Even if you ultimately get a publishing deal, it may be upward of eighteen to twenty-four months before the book actually lands on shelves. Therefore, money should not be your primary purpose in writing. Sure, that is the ultimate goal for anyone wanting a published book but it should not be your main focus.

Pay close attention to the writing styles of others you admire, not so that you can copy them but so you can understand that they actually exist. I understand my writing style and I admire the writing styles of many others. However, as a publisher, I have also received a lot of submissions from writers with no writing style whatsoever.

Speaking of books, I suggest that you take the time out to read some style manuals, like the *Chicago Manual of Style*. Brush up on the basics of grammar and punctuation if you need to. Even the best and the most educated of us are subject to forgetting the rules. Keep a dictionary and a thesaurus close at hand. You may be surprised by how much you have forgotten since grade school. If something is not practiced all the time, it can be easily forgotten. That is why parents who might've gotten straight As and Bs in high school math classes struggle to help their fifth-graders do their math homework. If you do not use it, you lose it.

CHAPTER 3

Outlining Your Story

The development of an outline can be one of the most important steps a writer can take to achieve a great end result. A lot of writers end up with storylines all over the place without one.

Outlining a Nonfiction Book

Nonfiction books cover a plethora of topics, from art, architecture, photography, and design, to technology, transportation, and engineering, to religion, science, and psychology—and everything in between. Then there are self-help books on improving everything from your health and physical well-being to selecting the right fashions and the right mate. In addition, there is a huge literary arena for memoirs, autobiographies, biographies, and family history books.

The first thing that one should do once the decision is made to embark upon the process of writing a book is to decide on the intended "take-away" from the book. What is it that you want readers to understand, appreciate, or learn from your book? I will take a few of the aforementioned topics and tell you how to outline them.

I am often approached by people who want to write their life stories. They feel like the world needs to know what they have endured, overcome, and/or achieved and how they were able to do it. For those who have led troubled lives, the act of writing could be about the personal healing process. Instead of journaling in private, they want to expose their journey and hopefully help someone else along the way. The best way to outline a memoir is to think of your life as a series of windows. Each window allows the reader a view of a pivotal moment or time in your life that altered who you were or who you have become. If you had to break your life up into twelve to fifteen windows, what would someone see when they look through them?

Let me give you a fictional example:

Angelina is a fifty-six-year-old Brazilian female who immigrated to the United States when she was eight years old after both of her parents were brutally murdered in a political uprising. She managed to escape with the family of her best friend, Cecilia, to California. Angelina was abused by Cecilia's older brother from the time she was ten years old and for the next four years before she ran away, finally opting to take refuge in the chaos of the streets rather than deal with the sexual molestation at home.

Angelina was abducted and forced into sex trafficking from then until she was twenty-one. She was treated like an animal—raped and mutilated—by a man named John who she initially thought she could trust. Angelina found herself walking into a church late one night, not sure why she was drawn to it, and met a priest named Father Peter. When he asked her what was wrong, she broke down in tears and told him her experience, specifically with John. Father Peter arranged for her to be relocated to another area of California where a friend of his, Michelle, ran a shelter for women. There John would never find her.

Michelle helped Angelina get her GED, and along with the other women in the shelter and the daily group sessions, taught her how to love herself and become self-sufficient. She joined with other women at the center to establish a small corporation, selling homemade hair and body products. Even though Angelina was not a chemist, she had developed a lot of financial savvy and helped to maintain the corporation so that profits were made.

The business became successful and profitable enough that the women were able to reestablish themselves in society. One by one, they began to branch out on their own and move away from the shelter. Angelina elected to stay there with Michelle to help run the center while maintaining the business and teaching the new residents how to make, package, and market the products, mostly via social networking. While Angelina was able to make positive changes in her life, her accomplishments didn't mean she wouldn't have to endure more pain. Michelle, her supporter and friend, developed breast cancer and died very quickly, leaving Angelina devastated.

Angelina took over the shelter completely, and to this day still runs it. She was fortunate to marry a wonderful man, a career military man, and together they have five sons and two grandchildren. Angelina ended up turning that small corporation into a nonprofit that became the largest organization for women in the world, allowing them to work, make money, and give back to those behind them. She has won numerous awards and is known for her compassion, humility, and intelligence.

So now Angelina wants to write a book, a memoir that will inspire other women to never give up on their dreams. The windows of her life would look something like this:

1. Angelina's earliest memories of her parents and her life in Brazil. How strong and loving her parents were and various activities they used to do with her. Her early childhood education and memories of her grandmother, who died when she was six.

2. The murder of Angelina's parents and the effect that their deaths had on her. The shock of it, the

fear of not knowing what would happen next, and being a young orphan in a hostile environment.

3. Fleeing to the United States with Cecilia's family, being an illegal immigrant, and the difficulties of enrolling in the school system, obtaining fake paperwork, and the glaring cultural differences between the two countries. Learning to speak English as a primary language.

4. The years of abuse, not being believed after telling on the brother, and how it affected her emotional well-being.

5. Running away, living on the streets, being approached by John and forced into sexual slavery.

6. The years of sex trafficking, the horrific things she experienced and witnessed.

7. Being drawn to the church that night and meeting Father Peter, his immediate compassion toward her, and the details of the conversation that ultimately saved her life.

8. The relocation to another city, meeting Michelle, and her interaction with other women in the shelter. Realizing that she was not alone, that none of

it was her fault, and that she had a support group of warriors in her corner.

9. Her transformation from being downtrodden to becoming educated, enlightened, and empowered.

10. The history behind the corporation: the premise, the purpose, and the birth of it.

11. Michelle's death and how it affected her. Angelina's decision to stay on and run the shelter and the corporation. The decision to convert it to a nonprofit.

12. Meeting her husband, falling in love, and the wedding.

13. Married life, the birth of the children, grandchildren, and maintaining a home life while steadily building an empire.

14. What the nonprofit has achieved, how it has changed lives forever, and where Angelina sees it going in the future.

15. Inspirational words of advice for other women struggling to find their way in life. A detailed affirmation of what is possible if one develops certain

traits, beginning with an incredible faith and the ability to overcome fear.

Those would be the windows and, ultimately, the chapters of Angelina's memoir.

Let's take a look at another fictional example:

Henry wants to write a book on the complete history of African-American inventors. Unlike a memoir, in which someone is discussing his or her own life and memories, this type of book often requires more research. And research is where it begins. There are the obvious ones that most school-aged children know about from textbooks: George Washington Carver, Madame C. J. Walker, and Garrett Morgan. Then there are the lesser-known inventors like Elijah McCoy, Otis Boykin, and Dr. Patricia E. Bath. Henry needs to decide what is going to make his book stand out from all of the others. Ultimately, the book will have to appeal to teachers and librarians since this book is meant to be educational.

So Henry decides that he is going to take on the task of writing mini-biographies of the inventors' lives, instead of simply mentioning what they invented. And he does not want to use the information on Wikipedia (not totally reliable because anyone can add information) or even data he can find in already published books. He is fascinated by the people and decides to compile a list of ten of them and dig deeper. Henry has his Masters in Journalism and he wants to combine his fascination with the subject of invention with his desire to be an investigator.

Henry decides that he is going to take a full three years to write the book. He decides on his ten subjects and tries to find some of their descendants, or in the case of younger inventors, some of the people who actually knew them. He decides that at least two of the chosen case subjects must still be living. So he decides on Janet Bashen, who was the first African-American woman to receive a software patent, and Lonnie Johnson, a NASA mechanical engineer who invented the super soaker.

His chapters are rather self-explanatory. Each one will showcase a different inventor, but he still has to decide how he will arrange the chapters. Will he do it based on the chronological order of their most famous inventions? Will he do it based on the regions of the country where they live / lived? Will he do it based on their genders? The world is his oyster, but what he needs to do is play around with all of the options and decide which one will be most attractive to readers and which one will make the book flow seamlessly. Most importantly, he needs to make sure the book starts with engaging material so readers will care to read the rest of the book.

Outlining a Fiction Book

When it comes to outlining fiction, there are many similar-ities to outlining nonfiction, but there are some differences as well. The most crucial thing is striking a balance between essential elements of the book and what I call "fluff." Fluff items are things added to a book to either make it humorous, dramatic, sensual, or shocking, but when it comes down to it, the storyline is not compromised or influenced by any of it. For example, a scene in which a character is listening to a particular famous singer or watching a popular reality show may strike a familiar chord with some readers but other readers might not care about it. Spending three pages giving the background of a nonessential character who will not even appear in the book beyond the current scene is a waste of time. I recall reading one popular book years ago where the author spent pages upon pages setting up characters that I presumed would turn into central characters, and then they were never mentioned again in the entire book. The book was huge and at least half of it was fluff material.

It is imperative to keep your storyline crisp, streamlined, and as straight-to-the-point as possible. If you are writing and realize that you are going way off into left field, even if it is a good concept, you may want to consider storing that away for another project. That is the beauty of writing fiction. You can come up with creative concepts and you can use them wherever they perfectly fit. I have often done that myself; I've thought of a great idea but realized that it had nothing to do with what I was writing so I emailed the idea to myself to use later.

As for the actual outline, I will use one of my own novels as an example instead of presenting a fictionalized scenario.

In my novel, *Total Eclipse of the Heart*, one of the few novels that I outlined before I wrote it, there are three sections of the book: The Lunar Eclipse, The Solar Eclipse, and The Total Eclipse.

In the first section of the book, Damon and Brooke do not know each other from holes in the wall. They both reside in the Washington, D.C., area but have never met, though they live somewhat parallel lives. They are both in toxic relationships (Brooke with her live-in attorney boyfriend, Patrick, and Damon with his wife, Carleigh). Both of them have lying, disrespectful, unsupportive mates who talk down to them, chip away at their self-esteem, and basically put themselves before Brooke and Damon. So the readers get an eagle-eye view of the drama, disappointment, and deception that both of them have been enduring.

In the second section of the book, Damon and Brooke find themselves thrown together in the wrong place at the wrong time when they're involved in a car accident. Damon saves Brooke's life in the process of saving his wife's life, but he loses an arm. Now, this is where things heat up. In the aftermath of the tragedy, Carleigh treats Damon like a new vehicle with a dent on the bumper because of his disability, and she appears ashamed to be married to him. Brooke, on the other hand, showers him with praise and gratitude for being her savior. Damon and Brooke develop a close friendship and begin to see traits in each other that are obviously missing in their respective mates, like their mutual supportiveness. Carleigh and Patrick continue to engage in more and more foolishness, yet Brooke and Damon continue to go around the mulberry bush, trying to make their obviously dysfunctional relationships work.

In the Total Eclipse section of the book, Brooke and Damon both start to recognize that they have fallen in love, despite all their efforts not to go there. So they begin to face their shared dilemma. Neither one of them wants an extramarital affair, yet neither one wants to hurt the feelings of their respective mates and end things. Nonetheless, the sexual tension between them grows thick. After a close call in a hotel room, they decide to part ways and end their friendship. Each of their relationships ultimately falls apart, allowing Brooke and Damon—now single—to end up together and happily married in the end.

Now you can take a storyline and outline it chapter by chapter, or you can do it section by section as I did with *Total Eclipse of the Heart*. My outline went over all of the various milestone moments that needed to occur in each section, such as the tragic accident that served as the catalyst for their meeting in the second section.

What you need to do is similar: you need to decide the key moments and scenes in the book that will make the story come together and engage the reader page after page. The "fluff" material will come into play when you are rewriting, when cute ideas pop into your head. Be careful not to go overboard with the fluff. I cannot stress that enough. Fluff material also includes going overboard with detailing the scenery, giving a bunch of designers free publicity without the benefit of any kickbacks, and going off on random tangents about political and societal issues that have nothing to do with the topic of the book. If you feel the need to "go off" about a particular court trial currently happening or the amount of attention a celebrity with no talent is receiving, write a blog about it or a Facebook post and call it a day. There is a time and a place for everything and a fictional novel is not the place for making profound statements about your personal beliefs and feelings. Sure, everything in the novel needs to be based on topics of concern to you, but to give a speech on something is way too much and completely inappropriate.

Outlining a Screenplay

The most crucial element you need to concentrate on when it comes to outlining a script is time. Other elements are significant as well, like budgeting and production timelines, but timing is most important. When I say "time" I am referring to air or screening time. Clearly, on television, there is a time limit involved. Most shows are either in thirty- or sixty-minute time slots. Therefore, your script has to fall within those parameters. If you are writing a thirty-minute cable show with no commercials, you are talking about roughly a twenty- to twenty-five-page script. If you are writing a thirty-minute show for a network where commercials will be aired during your show, that page count drops to roughly eighteen to twenty-three pages, depending on the type of show and the balance of dialogue vs. action.

When it comes to sixty-minute cable shows, the script should be between fifty to fifty-five pages long and for a network, forty to forty-eight. These numbers are all circumstantial, depending on the aspects of each show. I will discuss that more later. A sixty-minute show usually consists of a teaser, four acts, and a tag. A thirty-minute show usually consists of a teaser, two acts, and a tag. When I say acts, I am not saying the parts that are shown between commercials because there will generally be more commercial breaks on a network. I am saying acts as in parts of the script that have some kind of transitional element between them.

Let's take a fictional example:

This sixty-minute show is called *Life Without Borders*. It is about two couples from totally different cultures who are forced to share a household because of the economy. Virtual strangers to one another, they have to find a way to get along. So the pilot episode might go something like this:

Teaser: Brian Taylor and Chester Mills meet at a financial crisis support group for top-level executives who were recently let go because of overseas outsourcing. The two men share their stories in the group and are immediately drawn to each other.

On network television, this would normally be followed by the opening credits and then a commercial break. On cable, generally, the opening credits. Some shows select to show the credits before the teaser to jump right into the story. In that case, they would use a transitional sequence after the teaser to move forward, such as showing flowing traffic or the outside of someone's house.

Act One: Brian and Chester are now at a local bar, drowning their sorrows in cheap scotch and discussing possible solutions to their financial woes. Brian hesitates for a moment and then blurts out the suggestion that Chester and his family could move into the home he shares with his wife and kids. Chester is taken off guard but viewers can tell he is seriously considering it. After all, necessity is the mother of all inventions. The act ends with them parting ways and heading to their respective houses.

Act Two: This could be an act that moves back and forth between the two households as the men drop the idea of cohabitation on their wives. Viewers quickly comprehend that these two women are nothing alike and there is going to be a lot of drama if this plan is put into place. Brian's wife, Agnes, is a country bumpkin from Kentucky with little polish and she keeps their home in a chaotic state. Not dirty, but cluttered. Agnes allows their two daughters, Marilyn and Stacy, to run all over the place and do whatever they like. On the other hand, Chester's wife, Janice, is from Argentina. She is regal and keeps their home in immaculate order. She does not have a hair out of place and she is stern with their son, Phillippe. The viewer's anticipation rises after seeing the huge differences in their living environments.

Act Three: Brian and Chester meet back up in a city park

and discuss the situation further. They start talking about their families and both of them flat-out lie about certain things, e.g. when Chester asks Brian if his wife is a clean freak like his, Brian lies and says that she is. When Brian asks if his child is a free soul, Chester lies and says that he is. You get the picture. The two men decide that, despite the fact that their wives object, they are putting their feet down and making the arrangements for the move. As Brian leaves with the impression that Chester will have no issues paying half of his mortgage, Chester receives a phone call and it is made clear that Chester is not only broke, he has liens all over the place and is also facing possible embezzlement charges from his former corporation. Uh-oh!

Act Four: The two families come together at Brian's house for a lovely dinner that becomes anything but once the two wives lay eyes on each other. Agnes immediately develops self-esteem issues when she sees the beautiful, not-a-hair-out-of-place Janice. Janice is appalled when she sees the sloppily clad Agnes and her train wreck of a house. The two men try to pretend like none of this is a shock to them and the poor kids do not know what to do or say. It is clear, however, that Brian's kids will run all over Chester's son. Agnes asks to speak with Brian privately in the kitchen and Janice asks to speak to Chester privately in the yard and the arguments ensue.

Tag: This is a quick segment showing the wives back in the house, pouting and sighing as the men act excited about the new living arrangements. Yes, this show is turning out to be something else, and viewers cannot wait to see what happens next.

The tag will be followed by either scenes from the next episode and the ending credits, or simply the ending credits if there is no preview.

That is the basic thought process for outlining a script. I will explain film scripts later.

The Bottom Line

The way that you choose to outline your story can ultimately make it or break it. Rarely will you get a pass or a second opportunity to have the attention of a decision-maker in the business—not with all of the competition in the writing market. Take your time and commit to doing the best.

CHAPTER 4

Character Development

Write out character sketches before you even begin your project. Understand who they are, how they think, where they come from, and what they have experienced. In addition, the same needs to be done about their current stages in life. I keep a separate file for every book that I can refer to as I'm writing. I add to it as needed when I reveal more details about the characters in the book.

Outside of having some overall writing talent and proficiency, the ability to develop powerful and unforgettable characters is at the top of the list for capturing the attention of readers. A storyline or plot is one thing. Most people have a good enough imagination to come up with an interesting story, but to breathe life into the storyline is what matters.

That begins and ends with the readers harboring concern and/or feelings for your characters. An excellent writer, whether of fiction, nonfiction, or the screen, pulls at the heartstrings of those experiencing their work. Compassion, anger, empathy, hatred, disgust, fear, admiration, love; unless readers feel something for your characters, good or bad, the storyline will be meaningless.

So how do you develop your characters? By taking the time to define who they are. You must understand everything about your characters, whether or not all of those traits and facts end up in the final product. For example, on my cable series *Zane's The Jump Off*, the main character, Dmitri Vance, has a complicated life. He is the son of a single mother. His father died when he was younger but was never there for him in the first place, at least not until he became a professional football player. He was in love when he was younger but thought the young lady moved away to avoid him, though she actually moved away because she was battling lupus and was pregnant with his child. She did not want to ruin his chances of playing college football, and then later pro football for the NFL, so she left and begged her parents not to tell him about their son. She died and Dmitri did not find out about Harris, his son, until Harris had his adoption records opened at the age of eighteen.

Then Dmitri is forced to actually become a mature man, even though he is in his early thirties. All of his adult life has been a playground: millions in his bank accounts, women coming out of the woodwork trying to sleep with him, hanging out with his friends at his club during the off-season. The only thing that Dmitri ever took seriously was football. Once that is threatened by a potential career-ending injury, Dmitri realizes that he isn't as intelligent as his fraternity brothers, and even after a decade of playing pro, has never truly accepted that his career would one day end. He has no idea what he will do after his football career is over.

On top of trying to make amends with his son, even though he was never a deadbeat father, Dmitri finally gets a chance with the woman of his dreams, Lauren. But she is not willing to be another random broad that Dmitri entertains in his bed. He is going to have to prove himself to her; that means being patient.

Things do not go well at first. Brenda, Dmitri's "jump off," has visions of marriage and baby carriages and is not willing to go gently into that good night. He continues to sleep with her in the beginning but then dismisses her when he realizes that Lauren will never take him seriously until he does. For once in his life, sex has been moved to the back burner. But Dmitri has used Brenda, even though he never promised her anything. He knows that she loves him and he should have been man enough to give up the sex once it got to that point. Instead, he encourages her to keep believing she can change him by continuing to sleep with her on the regular.

Dmitri has even more issues with his friends. Woody, who manages his club, is angry with him because he has bent over backwards to appease Dmitri over the years, to his own detriment and to the point of losing his wife. Woody is a whiner, has always been a momma's boy, and has some apprehension about trying to succeed on his own, despite having an MBA that his wife, Kenya, paid for him to get. Once Kenya gets fed up with him and kicks him out, Woody does what most men would do when their egos have been bruised: he starts sleeping with various women to help himself get over it. It does not work.

Woody is extremely jealous of Earnest, their fraternity brother recently released from prison. He is jealous of Earnest's relationship with Dmitri, and at the same time, he wants to protect Dmitri from any trouble Earnest might bring into the fold. No matter what, Woody is going to give Earnest a hard time and accuses Earnest of being a moocher, even though Woody lives completely off of Dmitri, both by working in his club and living in his home.

Woody has a very immature demeanor, whether engaged in conversation with Kenya and accusing her of sleeping with her boss, or acting childish on the volleyball court and golf course simply because Earnest is around. Like Dmitri, he is forced to finally become a man when he realizes that he is about to lose his wife for good. However, Woody makes a lot of crucial mistakes in his efforts. Namely, not cutting off a "jump off" when it is apparent she desires more, and then lying to Kenya about whether or not he has slept around during their separation, even after she admits that she has. Woody will ultimately learn that bend-ing the truth rarely works and that blamers act like victims and victims cannot grow.

Earnest had taken the fall for his older brother, Chandler, a city councilman. As children, Earnest looked up to Chandler and followed his footsteps. After becoming a successful entertainment attorney, Earnest risked it all, including his private practice with his wife, Portia, in order to help his brother launder some money. The mistake was huge but one that he would not compound by allowing their parents to lose both of their sons to the system. So after five years in federal prison, Earnest has returned and is confused about a lot of things.

He had hoped that Portia, his true love, would have waited for him, but she divorced him and has a new man. He has to try to acclimate to society and cannot find a decent job with a felony on his record. He holds out hope on Portia for a while but is seduced by a married woman who frequents the club and ends up in a brawl with her husband that leaves Dmitri injured. Things begin to go downhill from that moment on. Earnest turns to drowning his sorrows in alcohol, which leads to running away from the world and suicidal thoughts.

Portia gets his hopes up by sleeping with him, but swiftly informs him that doing so does not mean she wants to reconcile. So what does Earnest do? He turns in anger toward the person behind all of this: his brother, Chandler. Chandler has always made him feel like the "lesser son" by implying that their father loved Chandler more than Earnest, by bragging that he will be the future mayor of Miami, and by distancing himself from Earnest when he could easily hook him up with a cushy job. Even when Earnest tries to warn Chandler about some of his associates trying to set him up, Chandler is more focused on talking down to him and making threats to Earnest to stay away from Sabrina, his wife. With retribution in his heart, Earnest seduces Sabrina, arranges for Chandler to get arrested for the sins of his past, and believes that it will all make him feel like a bigger man. Does it ever turn out that way?

Speaking of bigger men, Spencer is a six-foot-four Dominican radio personality who, like Dmitri, has remained single and ready to mingle his entire life. He considers himself to be the consummate playboy but always keeps one main "jump off" at the ready. Like Woody and Dmitri, he has led Jennifer on, not by making promises but by not cutting things off when she expresses that she desires more from him, and by refusing to respond to her questions about him sleeping with other women.

Spencer has a serious fear of commitment, even though he is constantly giving other men advice on how to make love last. The problem is that he needs a woman who challenges him, stimulates him intellectually, and one who will not back down from his foolishness. He has always had feelings for his cohost, Nandi, but she is so bitter toward men in general, and him in particular, that he has never been bold enough to speak up. However, when Nandi decides to participate in a reality show to find a man, Spencer goes through a range of emotions, from trying to have sex with Jennifer so he can keep his mind off of it, to ridiculing Nandi about the dates and hinting that he might be the one.

Spencer has to finally man up and lay his heart and feelings on the line, something he has never done. Maturity has come hard for him; he never truly left college in his head but he will move heaven and earth to prevent Nandi from lying down with another man. Spencer is finally forced into his manhood once the alternative, continuing to play a field that has long been overplayed, becomes less appealing than taking a chance at true love.

True love is exactly what Gabriel has with his wife, Aspen. Married for many years after being college sweethearts, they're now parents of two kids and holding down powerful careers—he as a financial advisor and she as the editor-in-chief of a major newspaper. The world is truly their oyster. But Gabriel has some double-standard issues that he needs to work on. He does not believe that a wife should be hanging out with her friends a lot, even though he spends tons of time with his fraternity brothers. He is insecure and begins to think that Aspen may be sleeping with her best friend for that very ridiculous reason. Even though he hangs out with his friends, he never does anything inappropriate. In fact, he is the one who keeps the rest of them grounded, having pledged them all to their fraternity in college.

Gabriel has a full-time job directing funds and a part-time job directing the lives of his friends. He views them as men who are coming into their own but are not quite there yet.

He is always the one telling people how to get it together, open up about their feelings to each other and to women. And he is the protector of them all—a huge weight for one man's shoulders. It does cause some tension between him and Aspen when he tries to convince her not to expose Chandler's affair. For a second, Aspen loops him in with all trifling men and he decides that he would rather stay in his lane than cause friction in his marriage. Gabriel is the strong, silent type, a hopeless romantic with a heart of gold.

So those are the five main characters of *Zane's The Jump Off*. I went through them for a reason. Most of the characteristics I assign to a character show up in the script and on the screen, but not all of them. Nonetheless, the characters— both male and female—appear well-developed both as a consequence of good acting and the information I've put into the script. I created a backstory for each character in *Zane's Sex Chronicles* and *Zane's The Jump Off*, and the director was able to explain the life histories of the characters to the actors portraying them. This is the information that allows a professional actor to not mimic, but rather *become* the character they're portraying and consequently convince an audience.

Backstory

Backstory is essential to understanding the characters in their present moment. The backstory can be concentrated into the beginning of the book, as it is in the first eighty pages or so of *Addicted* and in the first chapters of *Shame on It All* and *Afterburn*, or it can be scattered throughout a book, as it is in *Nervous*, *The Sisters of APF*, and *The Heat Seekers*. It can also be told in snippets, moving back and forth between the present and the past in the same chapter, with a character reminiscing about past events via internal monologue or dialogue. What it boils down to is making the reader understand how people became who they currently are and what the primary focus of the novel is, based on the thought patterns and prior actions of the characters.

Nothing irks me more than to get excited about a book, based on description alone, and then have my excitement deflated when I realize that I have no idea who the people are that I am reading about. Especially when people are doing things that are not typical behavior. It begs the question of why. Why would someone take another life and feel no remorse? Why would someone be willing to sleep with someone's spouse? Why would someone flip out in the middle of a grocery store and start cursing out complete strangers? Why would someone run out into the middle of rush-hour traffic? Why? Why? Why? That is what needs to be established with backstory.

Let us examine the two main characters in my novel *Afterburn*. Rayne Waters and Yardley Brown see each other in passing almost every weekday at the bank where she works. They are both attracted to each other, but for months neither one of them is willing to make a move on the other. Both of them have insecurities and doubt stemming from their respective pasts. Rayne's mother taught her at a young age that men are only interested in women for sex. She proved that by boasting about all of the men she had slept with, including the father of Rayne's best friend, whom Rayne always thought was the perfect husband. Rayne also relinquished her virginity to a young man she believed would be there for her, only to immediately get dumped. The list of her past heartbreaks went on and on, from the undercover homosexual she caught with another man at a party he'd invited her to, to the broke ex-convict who disgusts her every time she even looks at him. Her confidence in finding a good man is slim, and she also fears she will ultimately turn out like her mother. Unintentionally, she has slept with a lot of men. Not because she yearned to be a whore, but because none of them turned out to be who they professed to be. She has never truly opened her heart to a man, since she believes they will all cheat.

Yardley, on the other hand, falls in love and falls hard. He blew it with a young lady in high school, who he desired to be his forever, by sleeping with a prostitute at a party before her arrival. He never forgot the look of pain on her face and decided to spend the rest of his days trying not to ever hurt another female. Instead, they have all hurt *him* and run all over him like a weak man. He is at the point where he would rather just concentrate on his chiropractic practice, date casually whenever his friends beg him to double date, and accept the fact that no matter how hard he tries to do the right thing, he is constantly hooking up with the wrong women. One woman even left him for another woman.

When Rayne and Yardley finally start dating nearly halfway through the book, they are two damaged people hoping not to be damaged again. By the time readers get to this point, they understand why these two people are going to have a hard time opening up to each other. Readers feel compassion toward them because both Rayne and Yardley want to find the true love they deserve. And later, when tragedy strikes, the tears flow. I cannot begin to tell you how many readers have emailed me over the years, or approached me at events, or told the entire crowd how much *Afterburn* affected them emotionally. One person emailed me to say that she was going back to school because life was too short for regrets, another emailed me to tell me that she planned to make amends with her father after many years of no communication. All of that came about not because of the storyline but because of the characters and how readers were attached to them.

I once read a book about a woman whose boss would break into her home on almost a weekly basis and rape her. Now, while that might seem shocking, it did not move me to feel too many emotions for the woman because her character was not developed enough for me to feel anything. Backstory was lacking. I wanted to know why a woman would endure that and then go to work and act like nothing happened. It is plausible for it to happen, but only if the woman has something in her past that causes her to be scarred, e.g. if she has been abused, if she has mental issues—something.

My point is that her behavior is not normal, so there needs to be an explanation as to why it is occurring.

Back to Rayne from *Afterburn*. Even before I started the book, I had a complete sketch of her physical appearance, her educational background, her apartment in Georgetown, her financial savvy, her clumsiness, her current vehicle, her favorite restaurant; all of that mattered. If that sounds silly to you, then you may not be serious about the craft of writing. Sure, you can make up a name and call it a day. You can make simplistic statements about a person's background and hope someone cares. You can take every shortcut known to man and you will also come up short in appealing to readers. Take the time to formulate your characters and it will make a world of difference to the finished product.

As a writer, I can give testimony to the fact that my character development has garnered me the majority of my fans. As a publisher, I can definitely give testimony to the fact that there have been many books that sparked my interest based on the synopses but completely flatlined for me by the time I got to chapter three. The same thing happens in movies and with television shows with poor character development. I am sure that you could easily come up with at least a dozen movies that you were rushing to the theater to see based on the trailer and wanted to ask for your money back halfway through the movie. Yes, the movie had the things the trailer indicated. Something crazy happened, someone was in danger, and someone became the ultimate hero—the typical action flick. Now, it can go two ways: the audience could walk out pissed for wasting their money, or the audience could walk out praising it for being an awesome movie and whip out their cell phones to start texting and tweeting to their pack that it is a must-see. The difference? One version has all the action but no one gives a damn about a single character. The other version takes the time to develop the characters, so people gasp, twist in their seats, and possibly even shed a few tears over their predicament.

The Bottom Line

Characters are the meat and potatoes of writing. Without them, you have nothing. Even if there are no human beings in a book, even if the main character is a bird, a dragon, or an animated figure, they need to be vividly drawn and spark some type of emotion. You could keep a separate file open on the computer like I do, or keep a composition book with the details (something I have done in the past), or you can make up actual forms with preprinted lines (age, hair color, eye color, weight, height, car, career, etc.) and do one for each character. The point is, I am already living and breathing the characters before I start writing. Then all I have to concentrate on is the actual story.

Your main character must especially be strong and relatable. Whatever you do, do not give any of your characters what I call "The Cinderella Complex." Even though Cinderella is one of the most enduring characters of all time, in my opinion she is one of the weakest ones as well. If you think about it, Cinderella did absolutely nothing to move her life in any direction. Everything that happened in the story was because someone else, or something, caused it to happen. Cinderella simply went with the flow.

Think back to some of your favorite books and/or movies. Make a list of your top ten and then remind yourself why you included each one in the list. Sure, some of them might have had very strong and unique storylines, but if you truly analyze them, nine times out of ten one or more of the characters are the most memorable to you. Even when it comes to the extremely profitable action-hero movie franchises, the complexity of the numerous characters and the relatable nature of them is what makes the action that much more incredible. I have personally seen people shed tears and gasp when Batman or Iron Man faces imminent danger and possible death, even though everyone knows that they will ultimately save the day.

Your characters, especially the protagonist, should practically leap off the pages. Your readers should be hesitant to put the book down for even five seconds; they should yearn to know what is going to happen to the person next, what the person is going to do next, and how it will all end. All of that stems from the reader feeling like Angela, Randall, Susan, Michael, or Tonya—whoever the characters are—are sitting at their very dining room table. They should feel like familiar friends or relatives, people they know or used to know. They need to be "relatable."

CHAPTER 5

Writing Erotic Fiction

Being labeled "The Queen of Erotica," I could not possibly pen a book on writing and publishing and not include a section on writing erotic fiction.

For me, the sensuality is part of the overall story and not the main focus of the story. That is where I believe a lot of "erotic" writers go wrong. Like any other genre, character development determines whether or not readers will even care when something, whether positive or negative, happens to any particular character.

I will start with a little story. When I first decided to open up the floodgates to other writers and do an erotic short stories collection, *Chocolate Flava*, I received hundreds of submissions (which became the norm for all the collections that followed). There was one young lady who submitted a story that had some of the hottest sex scenes I had ever laid my eyeballs on. However, that was all there was: sex. Normally, I would have simply rejected her story, but I appreciated her imagery and the way her words flowed together, so I decided to send her an email. I do not remember what I said verbatim but it was something to the effect that I felt she had a lot of potential, but I wanted to know the following:

1. Who are these two people?

2. What are their backgrounds?

3. Who are they to each other?

4. Why would anyone care that they are having such amazing sex?

In other words, I told her to give it another shot and make me get caught up in the characters so I could understand the significance of the moment. The original story was about two people walking into a hotel room and immediately commencing sexual intercourse. Sometimes it gets down to that, but in this story I wanted to know why they were all hot and bothered for each other. The author had only alluded that they had not seen each other in a long time. Again, why was that?

I love when a writer is "coachable" and is willing to take

advice. The young lady emailed me back about a week later with an erotic story that was so hot, I actually made it the lead story in *Chocolate Flava*. It was the tale of a young woman who rode the bus to work daily and would often exchange inquisitive glances with a blue-collar man across the aisle. She wondered why he only admired her beauty but never spoke to her. She yearned for him to make any kind of advance toward her. Finally, after many months, he spoke to her but the excitement was quickly deflated.

As it turned out, he was a convicted felon who resided in a halfway house and was only allowed to leave the premises in order to go to and from work. They chatted for weeks on the bus before he decided he wanted to take her out on an actual date. He asked for special permission to miss curfew at the halfway house so they could spend some alone time together.

They ended up falling madly in love and both were looking forward to the end of his probationary period so they could be together full time and lie in each other's arms on a nightly basis. Then she received a dreaded phone call from him: he was picked up on a violation and would have to return to prison to serve out the remainder of his original time, plus a few years. The woman was devastated and deeply and emotionally attached to the man. She then became something she never expected: a prisoner's woman.

For the next five years, she waited for a different kind of bus on the weekends, the one that took women and their children up to the state prison to see their loved ones. Her friends and family members told her she was insane for waiting for him and spending her valuable time making that trek, only to communicate with him briefly from the other side of the glass.

So then we get to the big moment: the sex scene that was meaningless when I read it the first time. He is out of prison after five years, and they can make love after waiting so patiently and fighting so many feelings. Now the sex matters. Now it can resonate with readers.

That is the big difference between erotica and pornography—a question I'm often asked. Pornography—written or visual—is two or more people simply having sex, fucking, slapping skins (whatever one may wish to call it). Erotica is a story with real characters and real dilemmas. Erotica, even in short format, captures the reader's attention emotionally and intellectually. Let's face it, anyone can make two characters have sex! It takes a lot more effort to get you to feel for them. It is imperative that you have readers embrace everything about your characters, from their positive traits to their flaws. A lot of readers often complain about characters being "too perfect" in some novels and that makes them hard to relate to. Most people who are in love do not have perfect bodies, hair, teeth, etc. They are normal human beings and that means their looks, sizes, and issues vary. Reading about someone perfect having sex with another perfect person can get boring at times. I have published a series of erotic books by Eden Davis in which all of the main female characters are in their fifties. Fifty is the new twenty and that age range is when women are in their sexual prime. So what I am saying is, create "real people," not fantasy ones.

Over the past seventeen years, I have believed in creating characters that also happen to engage in hellified sex action. Roughly ninety percent of my short stories could have all of the sex removed, with some additional action and dialogue added in, and still be a full, rich story. The same goes for my full-length novels. I spend the majority of my time developing the characters, and then play out a story in my head, which ultimately ends up on paper. I develop their positive traits and their flaws. I examine their troubles and their ultimate ability to become empowered or liberated. I breathe life into them and they become a part of my household for a time. In other words, I make everything I write realistic, even when the characters are having the freakiest, out-of-the-box sex.

I am a very detailed writer and I do not tone that down when it comes to the sexual aspects of my stories. Why should I? People do not turn off some imaginary faucet when they enter their bedrooms and engage in intimacy. In fact, that is when people tend to feel the most alive. That is when all inhibitions are shed and two people feel so close to each other that they can practically feel the other person's heart beating in their own chest. At least, that is the way it should be.

The women I write about are the kind that a lot of women would become if they were not afraid of being judged. They engage in bold and brazen behavior that a lot of women crave to experience but religious principles, responsibilities, and old-fashioned values prevent them from indulging in. Great erotic fiction can liberate readers. I cannot count how many women have told me over the years that I am directly responsible for sexually liberating them. Many of them were in their forties or fifties and had never experienced an orgasm until they read one of my novels or short stories.

Most of my female characters are normal women who yearn for the love of a man and crave for him to make love to them like no other and, yes, sometimes fuck the shit out of them. They want to feel special, like they matter to another human being enough for him to make sacrifices for them. As I often say: "Lust is the benefit of self at the expense of others. Love is the benefit of others at the expense of self."

To me, erotica takes the more conservative romance novel to the next level. Consider a traditional romance storyline, one in which the heroine is single but the hero is involved with someone else, and the characters can't get together right away. There's a sex scene every eighty to ninety pages and there's no profanity. Instead of using words like "member" and "tool," you use words like "cock" and "dick." Or in my case, "mandingaling." Instead of using words like "flower" and "honey pot," you use words like "cunt" and "pussy." Or in my case, "cooter." Instead of using what I consider to be "safe terms" to describe intimacy, you actually let people "fuck." My point is to be descriptive the way people are actually descriptive in real life so that readers can imagine themselves in a similar situation—or can recall a similar situation from their past. Everyone likes to remember their greatest sex sessions. Try to get them caught up so that they do. Write about things that they have done, have contemplated doing, or wish they would have done prior to settling down with someone who may not be as adventurous. Make their toes curl and have them squirming in their seats—or beds—as they read your pages. I have long ago lost count of the number of women who have told me stories of masturbating in airport parking lots or at their jobs after reading one of my sex scenes. That is how you know you are making an impact. If in doubt, call someone you trust, or invite him/her over and read your scenes out loud to see what the person's reaction is. If there's little reaction, you need to return to the drawing board. If the person's eyes glaze over and you can see they are actually aroused, you are on the right track. If you're on the phone and they start breathing heavier, kudos to you and keep up the great work.

In my very first book, *The Sex Chronicles: Shattering the Myth*, I put a disclaimer in the front that went something like this: *If you are sexually repressed, oppressed, or have any sexual hang-ups whatsoever, please put my book down because it is too damn hot for your ass.*

I was not being sarcastic, actually. I was being realistic. I understood then and recognize even more now that everything is not for everyone, and that includes erotic fiction. Yet, I make no apologies for it. In all honesty, most of the contributors to my various anthologies are extremely intelligent and successful people. They come from all walks of life, from psychiatrists and surgeons to college professors and attorneys. They are very high-energy people who also enjoy great sex, unbeknownst to many who know them in their professional lives, which is why most use pen names. They want to be able to freely express themselves without the backlash. That is one reason why I enjoy publishing seemingly unknown authors instead of high-profile ones when it comes to erotic short stories. Those with reputations to protect often ride the fence when it comes to truly exposing their wild side. When you can hide behind a fictitious name, it helps to alleviate those issues.

Once you allow yourself to cross over any self-imposed boundaries and express your actual thoughts and desires, it can be an amazing ride. I am not saying that I do not enjoy what I consider to be typical erotic stories. What I am saying is that I have done live readings before with other erotica writers and when it came to my story, people were actually shocked—even the other writers. A lot of that is likely due to the fact that I never set out to write erotica; all I do is write the way that I visualize things.

Speaking of visualizing things, it is not necessary to only write about things you have actually done. Prolific writers who pen thought-provoking tales about aliens and monsters have never seen any. Mystery writers who spin engaging, graphic stories about serial killers and rapists do not engage in that kind of behavior themselves. So there is no reason why you have to engage in every single sex act that you describe.

Case in point: right now I am writing a novel that involves a woman who is so damaged by her past that she cannot stomach the thought of actual human touch. Thus, she is a dominatrix who commands other people—her human pets—on how she wants to watch them have sex. She only has sex with inanimate objects herself. Believe it or not, there are people just like her in the world. I was fascinated with the concept and chose to write about it. I wanted to examine how a woman could have such a high sex drive to the point that she orchestrates lewd sex acts among others and masturbates on a daily basis, but will not actually allow a man to touch her. To add to it, she is a famous celebrity who every straight man on the planet wants to take to bed and she is surrounded by fine men day and night. Yet, she cannot even imagine doing anything with them.

My challenge—and I love to challenge myself when it comes to writing—is to take readers on a rollercoaster ride that transcends both the mental and physical, ultimately liberating them from their demons altogether. You see, most negative behaviors—especially destructive ones—are symptoms of much deeper problems. It may seem strange for me to bring up such things in a chapter about how to write erotica, but the fact of the matter is that I tend to write about complicated women. Why? Because life is complicated and many of my readers are dealing with sexual hang-ups that are predated by something else.

My ultimate goal is to provoke thought and introspection for those who read my books and watch my shows, films, and my plays. I want something to resonate within them and not simply in their loins. The way we approach intimacy is directly related to the way we approach life itself. When you sit down to write erotica, take all of the aspects of your characters into account. If a person is an artist, they will be more creative in bed. There is a reason why a lot of the hottest erotic stories involve singers, painters, actors, etc. If a person is a heavy thinker, like a scientist, they will be more methodical when it comes to making love. If a person uses sex as an escape mechanism, they will tend to throw more caution to the wind and disconnect emotionally from their lovers, determined to make it all about the physical. Terms like "friends with benefits" and "booty call" are popular now because so many actual believe they can disassociate themselves from their feelings when it comes to sex—women, in particular.

Men, on the other hand, can do that very thing, and are practically bred to feel that way. Writing from a male point of view when it comes to erotica is a different challenge and one that I totally embrace. A lot of writers lose a level of comfort when it comes to writing in both genders. Obviously, I do not know what it feels like to stick a dick into a woman's pussy, or how the inside of her body feels. I do not know what it feels like to get a blow job with a breath mint in the woman's mouth. I do not know what it feels like to jack off. However, that is where having a vivid imagination comes into play. It is all about finding your own voice.

The Bottom Line

Do not spend so much time concentrating on construct-ing sex scenes that you overwhelm yourself with worry about what other people will think. That is the beauty of "fucking": creativity is king! Do not get hung up on what readers might think about it, either. So what if they do not agree with what your characters are doing within your pages? As long as they are reading it, that means they are getting something from it. Otherwise, they would put it down.

I am not going to go into too many graphic details in this book because I want it to remain a vehicle for everyone to learn about the writing and publishing processes. However, if you want to study my style, you have dozens of books that will spell it out for you. If I had to sum my writing style up in one word, I would have to say it is "innovative." I choose to march to the beat of a different drum and not emulate anyone else. It is better to make our own path and leave a trail than to follow someone else. Let all of your in-hibitions float out the window and have fun. Do it whether someone else ever reads it or not. Join some erotica online communities and vibe with other like-minded individuals. But most of all, remember to develop your storyline and characters. Even if it is a 3,500-word story, you can still en-gage your readers in who your characters are, and who they are to each other.

CHAPTER 6

Avoiding Typical Mistakes

Basic Spelling Errors

The most unbelievable mistake a writer can make, at least for me, is the misspelling of proper nouns. Someone actually turned in a book to me with the name of President Barack Obama spelled incorrectly. Yes, for real. I would say that at least half of the authors under my imprint turn in books with several misspelled proper names and places. We live in the age of the Internet. There is no excuse. Take five seconds and Google a name to double-check. If you are going to use the name of a college like Spelman College in Atlanta, please do not type Spellman. I have seen that in at least a dozen books over the years. If you are going to reference Men's Wearhouse, spell it correctly instead of saying Men's Warehouse. If you are going to use the brand—not merely the name—of a famous singer, actress, actor, or professional athlete, have the decency to make sure you spell their names right. This happens a lot of with the names of wine, restaurants, historical landmarks, you name it. Also, double-check about accents in someone's name. You cannot honestly expect readers to respect anything else you have to say if you make such careless mistakes.

A Few Grammar and Punctuation Notes

You should read *The Chicago Manual of Style*—the industry standard—and familiarize yourself with the correct formatting for songs, movies, TV shows, etc. For example, some tend to put song titles in italics when they really should be in quotation marks and not italicized. To give you a quick list, the following should be either underlined or italicized: a book or play, a periodical, a film, a CD or album, a reference book, and a television show. The following should be in quotation marks: an article from a periodical, an article or story from an anthology, a short story, a single song from a CD or album, a poem, and a single episode of a show.

Speaking of quotation marks, don't place punctuation outside of them:

"What did you say"?
"I cannot leave the office right now", she said.
"It is hotter than hell out here".

I am sure you get the point.

Moving right along, it is amazing that a lot of writers do not understand the correct way to list more than one character in a sentence.

Wrong way: *Me and Sally went to the store.*
Right way: *Sally and I went to the store.*

Wrong way: *Want to go to the movies with David and I?*
Right way: *Want to go to the movies with David and me?*

To make this easy, the sentence should read however it would if only the main person were present. You would never say, "Me went to the rodeo," or "It is too rainy outside for I to play?"

Using a random apostrophe is not a good look. Yet I see people do it all the time, not only in manuscripts but in emails. For instance, "album's" instead of "albums," "card's" instead of "cards," or "stick's" instead of "sticks."

Do not use a bunch of exclamation marks in your manuscript. They are not necessary. Either state that the character is speaking loudly, that the character raised their voice, that the character is angry, or use an exclamation mark once. It takes away from the dialogue when every sentence ends with an exclamation mark.

Study general punctuation and when each mark should be used. And do not use ellipses all over the book. I had one author insist on doing that throughout her books. I did not pick up her later books because of it and her refusal to change.

Overusing Words

Avoid using repetitive words in a sentence or paragraph. If you need to use a thesaurus there is one built into Microsoft Word, which you can access by right-clicking your mouse over the word. Most words have plenty of synonyms that will make the writer seem more intelligent and educated. To use the same word over and over makes no sense. Also, if you said that someone was in Arkansas in the first sentence of the paragraph, there is no reason to make that known again in the second sentence. For example:

We moved to Arkansas with my uncle. He was employed as a mechanic in Arkansas. The weather was very pleasant in Arkansas.

As you can see, the second two mentions of the state are not needed. Repetitive words can be very irritating to readers.

Giving them information that they already know can be irritating.

Tightening up your writing is important. The use of the following terms are unnecessary 99.99 percent of the time in a book: *I mean, I know, I knew, she knew, he knew, he knows, she knows, I remember, I recall,* and *I guess.* First of all, if a character is speaking, the reader realizes that they either know, remember, recall, mean, or guess whatever they are doing. Memoirs are often plagued with these terms. If someone is writing a memoir about his or her life, readers understand that everything is based on what they know or remember. The statements also make a more powerful punch when they are stated with true conviction. So instead of saying, "I guess that she was wrong for hitting me," say, "She was wrong for hitting me," if that is truly what you believe, or if that is the point you are trying to drive home.

Because and *just* are hands down the two most overused words in books. Again, 99.99 percent of the instances of *just* can be removed or at least replaced with other words like *simply, merely,* or *only.* As for the word *because,* it is often used to combine two thoughts into one sentence, even though sometimes they read more smoothly when they are separate. For example, one could say, "I never go out after ten o'clock at night because I never miss the news on Channel Five." Or you could say, "I never go out after ten o'clock at night. I never miss the news on Channel Five." Now, technically both are correct, but once you read the word *because* a dozen times per page, it quickly gets old and takes away from the book. The same goes for *just*. I have seen that word used up to three dozen times on a single page in a manuscript. That is way too much!

Misusing Words

Homophones are often traded for one another, especially when a writer is rushing, but also because a writer does not always understand which to use. If it is a homophone that is also a homograph or homonym—a word that is spelled the same but can have different meanings, like *rose*—that rarely matters in a book. However, if it is a heterograph, where a word sounds the same but has two different spellings, it is a huge issue. Some of the ones misused the most are: *your* and *you're*; *it's* and *its*; *there*, *their*, and *they're*; *principal* and *principle*; and *affect* and *effect*. If you are not sure of the differences in these words, please familiarize yourself with them so you can use them properly. Even though they are not homophones, people also use the words *use* and *used* wrong, especially *use*. Saying "I use to go to that school" is incorrect. It should be "I used to go to that school."

A lot of basic words are constantly misused by writers. Let me go over a few and clarify what they mean.

Then has many meanings but the main two are "in addition to" and "at a point in time."

Than is used to compare two different things, such as "my house is bigger than yours."

Loose means that something is "moving freely" or "not as tight as it should be."

Lose means "to misplace" or "to be deprived of something," such as losing a loved one.

Compliment refers to "something nice said about you."

Complement refers to "something that adds to or mixes with something in a pleasant way."

Fewer is used when you can count something.

Less is used when you cannot count something but you are still measuring in a sense, such as having "less opportunity."

Historical means something that happened in the past.

Historic means an important event, place, or person.

It's means "it is."

Its is a possessive term referring to something belonging to or specific about a certain person, place, or thing.

Flesh out means to give something substance.

Flush out means to try to lure something out into the open.

Into is a preposition that typically answers the "where" question.

In to might end up beside each other in a sentence such as, "I stumbled in to see both of them on the bed making out."

Toward and *towards* are both correct but *toward* is generally used with an American readership and *towards* is generally used with a British audience. It is a personal preference but I usually drop the *s* in the manuscripts that I edit.

When it comes to *who* and *that*, the word *who* should

always be used when referring to people. For instance, "All the neighbors who get there by noon will get a free toy." If you use *that*, you are generally referring to objects, and people are not objects.

Irregardless actually makes no sense and does not even appear in all dictionaries. The reason being that *ir* cancels out *regardless*. Just use *regardless*.

Centered around makes no sense either. You can be *centered on* something but not around it.

There is no such thing as a *mute* point. It is actually *moot* point, meaning that it is not worth discussing. This is a common mistake.

People tend to say that something *peaked* their interest when it is really *piqued*.

If you are trying to say that a character changed their ways, do not say that they made a 360-degree turn. That puts them right back where they started. It should be an 180-degree turn.

There is no such thing as *baited breath* but there is such a thing as *bated breath*.

Refrain from using the word *literally* unless it is an actual fact. In other words, do not say, "I literally felt like I was dying." Either something is dying or not.

A ton of writers are confused about when to use *that* and when to use *which* and the correct punctuation involved. Normally, there will be a comma before *which* because it is added to a thought that would not change the meaning of the thought if it were not included. *That* is necessary to complete the thought. Let us use the following as an example:

The Thomas house, which had dozens of windows, sat up on Mulberry Hill.

The Thomas house that had dozens of windows sat up on Mulberry Hill.

You may be asking yourself what is the difference and I am going to explain it. In the first sentence, the fact that the house has dozens of windows is irrelevant if the Thomas family only has one house. However, if they have more than one house, then it becomes important and the second sentence should be used. You are distinguishing the correct house by stating that it is the house with dozens of windows.

I will give you another example:

The puppies, which had black and brown spots, ran away from the kennel and were never seen again.

The puppies that had black and brown spots ran away from the kennel and were never seen again.

In this case, if there was only one set of puppies, the color of their spots would not matter. They all ran away. If only specific puppies ran away, then you should tell the reader which ones they were.

There is much confusion between *i.e.*, *etc.*, and *e.g. I.e.* stands for "id est" in Latin and means "that is to say." *Etc.* stands for "et cetera" in Latin and means "and other things" or "and so on." *E.g.* stands for "exempli gratia" in Latin and means "for example." So you could use *i.e.* in the following: "I like to read nonfiction; i.e. books with factual information." You could use *etc.* in the following: "I do not like any meats: beef, pork, chicken, etc." You could use *e.g.* in the following: "I love old movies, e.g. *Love Story.*"

For anyone who has written "for all *extents* and purposes" or "for all *instance* and purposes," it is "for all *intents* and purposes."

Please comprehend the difference between *to* and *too*.

Overusing Brand and Designer Names

While it is good to describe scenery and clothing in a book, too many authors take it to the extreme. You can simply say she was wearing a pair of red pumps without using a designer name, or she was wearing a black dress without attaching a label. If you choose to be specific, please double-check the correct spelling of the designer's name. There are two shoe designers in particular that authors often misspell. If you are trying to impress readers by making your characters well-dressed, at least spell the names right. The same goes for overkill on the description of surroundings. It is okay to say someone has a black leather sofa, glass entertainment center, and large flat-screen television. However, you do not need to describe everything down to the paperweight on their coffee table. This is a distraction from the story and it is not benefitting you or the reader. Recently an author turned in a book with a ton of designer names listed. He thought it was imperative to give readers a true understanding of the lifestyle of the characters. It was irritating to me and I spoke my mind about it. He insisted that readers would embrace it, but I would not be surprised if a lot of the comments and reviewers make note of it. Time will tell.

Switching Between Tenses

One of my biggest bones of contention is the misuse of tenses. I have honestly sat down to read a manuscript and been stumped on whether the writer intended the book to be in past or present tense. One book in particular jumped back and forth so much, sometimes in the same paragraph or even the same sentence, that the story's time was too difficult to determine. Anyone who understands the basics of writing should be able to pick a tense and stick with it. A sentence like, "She went to the store and parks in the handicapped space." Or a sentence like, "Donald used to drink all the time so I don't purchased any liquor." You have to select a tense and stick with it, at least where it counts. There are some authors who are great at moving back and forth between tenses and transitioning from backstory to a current timeline. James Patterson does this in many of his books. If you can do that and understand the concept, fine. However, most of the writers who jump between tenses are doing it because they do not understand the writing process, though tenses are part of the elementary-school level elements of writing.

Continuity

One of the most ridiculous things I've seen is when writers constantly spell the names of their central characters in different ways throughout the book. If you are going to pick a fancy name for a character, at least make sure that the spelling is consistent. I have read manuscripts where one character had her name spelled six different ways. I kid you not. It seems ridiculous for me to even have to point this out, but it has happened often enough. In fact, some not only spell the names differently but actually change the name altogether. Not a good look.

Similar to names changing throughout a book, it is imperative to make sure that your characters' looks remain consistent. I have seen books where someone had blue eyes in one chapter and brown eyes in the next. Or someone was a size ten and was suddenly shopping for a size sixteen dress. I mentioned this in the chapter on character development and I will stress it again here. Keep a detailed list of the traits of your characters. It is worth taking that extra few seconds to type or write it down. This includes their cars, styles of homes, etc. I have seen characters go from residing in apartments, to townhouses, back to apartments, and then in a rancher.

Point-of-view (POV) continuity issues are a huge problem in some books, especially those written in first person. Some writers will have a character describe a situation or conversation that they could not possibly know about in the first place. For example, one time an author turned in a book where the main character had gone outside to take the garbage out. Yet he was able to describe an entire conversation that his wife and mother were having as they did the dishes inside the house. The character even described their movements. That is impossible if he was nowhere near the conversation. If you find yourself stuck with a storyline issue because you need to try to get some information in to make your concept more fluid, this is where thinking outside of the box comes into play. You could have one of the present characters relate it to the main character later, but making it seem like he heard and witnessed it is a huge error. This is one reason why outlining a book is a good idea for more inexperienced writers.

Dialogue

He said, she said, and *I said* are completely overused in books. To me, it signifies a lack of creativity and maturity in a writer. A book should read like someone is watching a movie. In a movie, you would see someone perform an action (turning on a light, sitting on a sofa, walking across the room, getting something to drink) and then say something. But they just say it. They do not say it and then add, "I said." When you are writing a book, it may be helpful to write the dialogue out first and then go back and add in actions.

Typical way: *"I don't know what is wrong,"* she said *as she walked across the room. "He is usually home from work by now."*

Better way: *"I don't know what is wrong."* She walked *across the room. "He is usually home from work by now."*

I have often received emails from other writers complimenting me on the fact that I do not use those terms a lot. *I/she/ he said* is really not needed. I am not saying that it should never be used, but not in every single line of dialogue.

Right along those same lines: you don't need to constantly restate relations between characters. If you have already stated that Rachel is Mary's daughter, there is no reason to restate that every time that Rachel enters the story. I am shocked at how someone will do that over and over. "Rachel, Mary's daughter, was home from college for the summer." Skip a chapter. "Mary's daughter, Rachel, had never liked that particular restaurant." Skip a chapter. " 'I'm not sure what to do,' Rachel, Mary's daughter, said." The same holds true for reminding readers of a certain event over and over. For instance, if Harry and Len got into a fight in high school, you do not have to remind the reader of that every time they end up together. Give readers enough credit to remember that information.

A character cannot gasp, frown, chuckle, laugh, giggle, smile, or nod words. Amazingly enough, tons of characters in books do that very thing when someone writes, " 'I'm not even playing with you,' she laughed." It should read: " 'I'm not even playing with you.' She laughed." In addition to writing the above improperly, too many writers use the terms *chuckle, giggle, laugh,* etc. in the same conversation over and over. Once you set the tone for the conversation, it is not necessary to keep saying that the characters are laughing or smiling at one another. The reader understands that and it shows a level of immaturity in a writer to keep using the words over and over once the mood of the characters has been established. Unless there is a drastic mood change due to something that happens or something that is said, please refrain from the repetitiveness of such terminology.

It is important that you do not have all of your characters speaking in the same dialogue throughout the book. One of the signs of a weak writer is when all of their characters sound exactly alike. If one character has a tendency to say "whatever's clever" a lot, please do not have all of their friends, relatives, and coworkers using that same phrase. If someone says "it is what it is," do not have three other characters saying the same thing. Part of writing is being able to step outside of yourself, so even if you use those terms a lot, I am sure that all of those around you do not use them as well. If you need some help in this department—dialogue is a struggle for many writers—start to really pay attention to how various people speak during conversations. If you have to, call some of your friends up and have long talks with them and pay attention to how they each speak totally differently. Part of the development of a character is that person's voice, and that includes their dialect. If they are from a certain country or region of the United States, make sure they speak that way. If you are writing a book that takes place during the Civil War, study the way that people talked. Watch some movies from that time period, read other books from that time period. Take writing seriously. A lot of times when someone wins an Academy Award for Best Actor or Best Actress, it is for playing the role of a foreign or historical leader. They spend months, sometimes years, perfecting the dialect. Many of the major superstars in the United States are from foreign countries but they have perfected their American accent and can turn it on and off. You have to take writing dialogue as seriously as they do, even if you are not in front of a camera acting it out.

Similar to the above, you need to make the dialogue of your characters seem realistic based on their backgrounds, education, etc. Pick a lane and stay in it. Some writers will have a character speaking the King's English on one page and then in total slang on the next, often in the same conversation. Now I am not implying that most people do not have a separate professional and casual persona but I am saying that if a person speaks extremely well, they are not going to suddenly start using dangling participles. I have read at least a hundred books that had this same exact issue. You must give each character a realistic overall appearance, which includes their manner of speaking, based on the way that you create them.

Next on deck: writers having more than one character speaking in the same paragraph. Every time the speaker changes, you have to put it into a different paragraph. Make sure that the readers know which character is speaking. You are probably saying, "That is what 'he said,' 'she said,' and 'I said' is for." To that, I say, no, it is not. It is not even the time for "Mary said," "Tom said," or "David said." It goes back to having a character perform an action in the same paragraph so the reader knows who is speaking. When it is a conversation between two people, it does not need to occur in every instance of dialogue but you should add in something to specify which character is speaking at least every five to six lines. If there are more than two characters in the conversation, it would need to be cut to about every three lines.

Checking Your Facts (Even for Fiction)

Double-check geographical information. You cannot have characters going to a lake thirty minutes from the city where they live, or up into a log cabin in the mountains an hour away, if there are no such places within that vicinity. Yes, it is fiction, but readers do not want to be insulted. Also, they have a desire to get caught up in the moment. You have to remember that chances are—if you become even halfway successful—many of your readers will live in the area you are writing about. It means a lot to them for you to describe their hometown or home state in the way that it actually exists. If you have two characters going to Yellowstone National Park, take five minutes and go to the website and get descriptive material about the park and various activities available there to make it seem more realistic.

The same holds true when you use the names of restaurants, museums, etc. Please do not say that characters ate something that is not even on their menu. If you care enough to give that restaurant some free publicity, get it right. Even if you have never been there, look up their website, and if they have red velvet seats do not say they have black leather booths. If they serve soul food, do not say that someone ordered an Italian entrée. The beauty of the Internet is that it makes the life of a writer so much easier.

I would be remiss not to mention confirming the dates and timelines of historical events, movies, songs, technology, etc. If you are going to write a historical book, make sure that you do not have someone describing an event that has not even occurred yet. If you are doing a period book, do not have characters going to see *Scarface* at the theater prior to it being filmed, or ten years after it came out. If two characters are dancing to a song, make sure that song was already out. Do not have someone listening to "Like a Virgin" by Madonna in 1972; it came out in 1984.

The Bottom Line

If you want to write professionally, you need to master certain fundamental skills and be familiar with the rules. Creative writing is art, and artists can create great work by breaking rules—but you have to know them first. Reading often and widely can help you to recognize and identify patterns, proper punctuation, and correct grammar, and it definitely helps to increase your vocabulary. All of the things that I've covered here were probably taught to each and every one of you at some point in your lives in one of your English classes. You may have forgotten a lot of it, you may have assumed that you were using the words, terminology, and punctuation correctly, and if you are already published, your readers may have filled your head with praise and accolades because they enjoyed the overall storyline. No matter where you are in your career, you should strive to avoid typical writing mistakes.

CHAPTER 7

Writing in Different Media

Most writers are only proficient in one writing medium, but there are those of us who have written in various media and understand the differences. I have seen many authors struggle with writing screenplays. That mostly stems from believing they could guess how to do it and going for it. The same can be said for screenwriters or playwrights who assumed writing a novel is a walk in the park because of their vast experience in their main medium. Like everything else, you must actually study the proper formatting and learn the correct methods. There are no shortcuts to quality work.

Writing Fiction

Writing fiction is the easiest of all for me because it has the fewest limitations. In fiction, the characters can be whoever you want them to be, go wherever you want them to go; the sky is the limit. In fact, if you want someone to skydive out of a plane at twenty thousand feet, all you have to do is put that down. But you must put be able to describe the action in the context of the world and/or setting you have imagined for your story. If you want them to live in a sprawling mansion in Texas or in a remote cabin in Costa Rica, all you have to do is put that down. If you want them to be third cousins, twice-removed of the Queen of England, they can be. All you have to do it put it down. Your imagination can run rampant as long as you make the reader believe. You can birth people, kill people, have gladiator fights in an arena, grant someone the privilege of driving a million-dollar car—whatever you want.

There are a lot of freedoms in fiction but there are still many things you must do to make it compelling. You have to engage the readers in something immediately, from page one. Otherwise, you might quickly lose them altogether by the second or third chapter. There are way too many other options. You want to evoke something in them that makes them hesitate to even put the book down. In a perfect world, they will stay up into the wee hours of the night to finish it, turn off their TVs, computers, and cell phones, and get caught up in the world of your characters. How does that happen? This is how:

There has to be one main character in your book. The story has to have a point of view. Even if you write a novel where you are going back and forth in first person between two characters, like a romance told from the perspective of both the man and woman, one of them has to be the main character. I have written several novels in the voices of two or more characters, but there was always a main voice: again, a point of view. In *Afterburn*, the protagonist was Rayne. In *The Hot Box*, the protagonist was Milena. In *Nervous*, the protagonist was Jonquinette. In *Shame on It All*—told in three voices—Harmony was the protagonist. In *The Sisters of APF*—told in three voices—the protagonist was Mary Ann. In *Skycraper*—told in four voices—the protagonist was Tomalis. In *The Heat Seekers*—told in four voices—the protagonist was Tempest. The main character, also known as the protagonist, is the focal character of the novel. The protagonist does not have to be the first character introduced but should be introduced as soon as possible to make the storyline flow smoothly.

Now, the protagonist can be someone who readers immediately feel a lot of compassion toward, or it can be someone who immediately angers or scares people. In a children's book or science fiction book, the protagonist could be a pig named Wilbur or an alien named Trek. That choice is up to you.

The antagonist can be a person, situation, or problem/

difficult situation in a book. If it is a book about a woman being abused by her husband, he would be the antagonist. If it is a book about a young man who wants to swim across the ocean to get back to his parents, the ocean is the antagonist. If the book is about a princess who is trapped in a dungeon by an evil witch, the witch is the antagonist, and so on.

Your book can be as short or long as you want it to be, but you do not want to turn readers off by making it seem like they are not getting enough material for their money, or making it seem like it will be too overwhelming to read because they are having flashbacks to school textbooks. For novels, the industry standard is around seventy thousand to eighty thousand words. People get away with less and people get away with more. Anything over one hundred thousand words becomes a monstrous tome. Editing costs shoot up, printing costs shoot up, and therefore, retail costs go up. It can be hard to convince readers to pay for an expensive book unless they are already a huge fan of yours.

All of the characters have to possess some kind of flaw. Perfect characters are hard to connect and relate to; they are a major disappointment for readers. They need to incite thoughts, shock, or laughter in people. They need to be independent and distinguishable from the other characters in the book. This holds true for scripts as well.

Have you ever started reading a book and found yourself skipping over certain parts to get to the juicy parts? You need to attempt not to include any parts of a book that your readers will want to skip over. That includes long, descriptive scene establishment. If it is raining outside, say it is raining and move on, unless there is something about that rain that drives the story and is critical to the story. No need to go through a three-paragraph explanation of how dark the clouds are, how the weatherman had called for less than an inch but at least four inches have fallen, how the sun was out earlier in the morning but now it has disappeared. We get it; it is raining.

Suspense, Surprise, and Plot Twists

It is always good to give the impression that a plot is going in one direction and then surprise the readers by going in a totally different one. I enjoy catching my readers off guard. Some of them get upset with me for years because of it. They'll be trudging along, reading a romantic love story, when suddenly the main character dies or is murdered. Another character appears out of the blue and blows up the spot with surprises, or starts spilling family secrets. The main character discovers he is being betrayed by someone he trusted with his life. The most charming, seemingly stable character turns out to be a serial killer. You get the point: do not be predictable.

Writing for Your Audience

Now I realize that there is a market for certain kinds of "formulaic books" where the heroine falls in love with the hero and they live happily ever after. Some readers want to keep it that simple. They want two sexy people on the cover and reassurance about how the book will end. The hero and heroine will meet, start courting, and experience a little bit of drama from friends, relatives, or past lovers, but they will inevitably end up together, married, and in a house with a white picket fence. If that is what you aspire to write, so be it. Many romance publishers have specific guidelines that break the storyline requirements down even further.

If you are writing a young adult novel, you need to make sure that you do not overstep certain boundaries that will dissuade parents from allowing their children to read it, including sex scenes and swearing. If you are writing science fiction, even though the storyline is obviously something that will likely never happen, you still have to try to make it sound believable enough for readers to buy into it. If you are writing erotica, you need to make sure that there are sensual elements in the book and that people are allowed to have some degree of understanding and compassion toward your characters. Otherwise, who cares if they are having sex? Readers will not care about anything if they do not care about your characters. I cannot stress that enough.

The key is to understand what audience you are trying to write for. Then again, some writers, like myself, do not write for a particular audience. We write and let the audience develop around the book, which is another option.

Writing to Develop a Series

If you anticipate writing a sequel, you need to set it up that way but also close the book out enough in case you never get around to it. If you are writing a mystery, you need to make sure that you leave enough clues for readers to go back and try to figure out how they missed them. Don't make the clues obvious, though, or else the reader will be ten steps ahead of you and upset when the ending turns out the way they predicted before they even reached the hundredth page. Avid mystery readers want to be taken off guard. If you fail to do that, they probably won't pick up any more of your books.

All in all, fiction is a literary playground. You should have some subplots in your book but do not make them too complicated or stray too far off the path. That changes somewhat as we move along to the other writing mediums.

Writing Nonfiction

Strong storytelling is just as important to nonfiction as fiction. The same characteristics apply to successful writing no matter whether the story is real or imagined. Nonfiction, of course, depends more on good research than stories that spring from the imagination of the writer.

In nonfiction, you need to answer one simple question to define its category: who would be the reader of this book and why? Is it self-help? Motivational? Educational? Inspirational? Self-help books must contain clear-cut instructions on how a person can get from point A to point B. They are meant to help you solve a particular problem or learn a particular skill, which could include weight loss, crocheting, reducing household clutter, or planting an herb garden. By the time your readers finish the book, they want to feel like an expert on the subject and be able to set about accomplishing whatever tasks you covered.

Motivational books are written to convince readers that they can overcome some kind of obstacle, negative emotion, or bad habit to achieve something. That includes forgiving those who have hurt them, having too much emotional baggage from prior relationships, or quitting smoking cold turkey.

Most nonfiction books stay on track with their purpose. However, memoirs can quickly go into left field. Even if a person is talking about their childhood and early years, there need to be tidbits of wisdom interspersed throughout the book that readers can apply to their own lives. I realize that a lot of people want to get their story out, and most say that they believe their stories can help other people. The key is you have to actually specify how your story can help other people. No one else has lived your same exact life, or the same exact life of whomever you are writing about if it is a biography. No matter how fascinating a life has been, people want to be able to somehow relate certain things to their own lives.

Also, when writing, help readers out by explaining references to people and things they may not know. Don't make them run to a computer to look things up. For instance, if you talk about someone who was important in your hometown, explain why. Was he the mayor? Was he from the oldest and wealthiest family in the area? Did he give a lot of teenagers summer jobs on his farm? Did he distribute turkeys during the holidays?

If you discuss a certain book or poem that made a profound change in your life, explain why. Did the work make you think of your own situation and how to overcome it? If you talk about how you would have the most fun when you visited your grandparents during the summer, explain why. Did your grandfather take you fishing every Saturday? Did your grandmother make you ice cream sundaes every night? Did you enjoy playing with your cousins and other kids in the neighborhood? Explain anything and everything that the reader will not automatically know.

Be careful, though, not to burden your story with stuff that veers away from the main focus. Just because a book is autobiographical or a memoir does not mean that every aspect, object, or person in your life needs to be mentioned. Do not feel that you have to go over every year in school from kindergarten to high school graduation.

You are going to have to decide where and how to make time jumps in the book. Once you complete your memoir, go through it and see what can be eliminated. Like I said before, do not leave anything in your book that would make readers want to skip that section to get to the parts worth reading.

Legal Issues: Libel, Slander, Etc.

In addition, if you are writing certain types of nonfiction for a major publishing house, the book has to be vetted through the legal department. If there is anything in there that can be determined to be libelous, malicious, or defamatory, it will be removed. Publishers are not going to risk a lawsuit, no matter how amazing the book may be. What you do not want to happen is for your book to be cut down so much that it is no longer publishable. Normally, a publisher will have some idea about those possibilities before they even acquire a book. If the manuscript is already written, that makes life so much easier. That way, everyone knows immediately whether or not the book will pass muster.

Writing for Television

Most television series have a creator, who generally writes the pilot episode of a concept, along with the show's bible. The bible of a show includes the overview of the series, the detailed information on all characters, and other pertinent information. There is generally an episodic breakdown of the season that the staff writers—generally who work in-house—use to complete the other scripts. Sometimes the creator will write the entire show, which has been the case with me in both instances. It depends on whether or not the person can handle the workload and the network is comfortable with one writer for the entire series.

What's Real in Reality TV?

There has been an explosion of reality television shows. Believe it or not, most are partially scripted. It is too risky for a network/production company to simply put a bunch of people together—no matter how animated their personalities are—and expect them to do what it will ultimately take to get the viewers emotionally invested in the show by the third or fourth episode. Therefore, there are writers who develop certain situations to place the talent in. There is a casting process, even for the minor roles, and if the talent does not make it interesting enough, their scenes could get cut from the final product—or they could be kicked off the show.

Here's a fictional example. There is a show called *Past, Present, and Future*, in which five bachelors are placed into a house together for three months. They are from various walks of life but all are attractive and somewhat successful. Each one of them has to go on dates with a female he dated in the past, the female he is currently dating, and a female who is interested in taking over. Throughout the season, viewers will see these seemingly thirsty women come and go from the house, seeking the attention of the man of their dreams.

So that would be the overall vision of the show, but it is too predictable. Therefore, the writers will have to spice things up by telling some of the women and men to go after someone who they are not supposed to be hooking up with, setting up scenes for a woman to walk in on her man kissing another woman, and staging catfights between the women by the pool area where their bikini tops are ripped off and their breasts are blurred out, which makes the audience members wish they were there to see the real thing. The talent is given topics of discussion, told to do a little pushing and shoving, insulting, instigating, and insinuation. You get the picture. The formula works well and tens of millions of viewers are glued to the screen weekly.

Scripted Programs

Also keep in mind that you have to grab the viewers' attention right away on television or they will quickly switch the channel. Your teaser (discussed previously in the outlining chapter) better be amazing. Your tag, or last act, better be amazing as well so they will be craving to tune in next week. The hard part about writing for television is carrying several character storyline arcs over numerous episodes (six to twenty-two) and still making each episode stand-alone enough that if someone happens to catch it, they will enjoy it and understand what is going on.

This is what I do: I sketch an overview of the season, with a brief outline of what will happen to each character throughout that season. Then I study those for a while and develop an episodic breakdown that spaces out the most dramatic revelations and milestones so not too many of them are happening in the same episode or consecutive episodes. Then I take the pilot episode and break it down into about twelve to eighteen scenes for a thirty-minute show. That needs to be doubled for a sixty-minute show. That sounds like a lot of scenes but it is not, because larger scenes are broken down into smaller ones.

You cannot have two characters holding a four-minute conversation on screen at one time. That is way too long, so what you do is have them start the conversation in one scene, cut to some other characters doing something else, possibly even two other scenes involving other characters, and then come back to the original ones and finish the conversation. So when I say twelve to eighteen scenes, there may really be six locations / situations split into two to three sections each.

Then it is time to worry about the page count. Each page averages about a minute of screen time. Of course, that is not always the case, but it tends to balance out in the end. If the show runs over the allotted time in editing, it will have to be trimmed without losing any of the key elements. I will be the first to admit that I have had to agree to losing a lot of really great footage in order to trim an episode by three to four minutes. It happens, but it is better to have too much footage that needs to be cut down than not having enough footage.

That brings me to a very important topic: dialogue being too wordy. A bunch of writers have sent me scripts to read and the dialogue is way too much. If a novelist decides to write scripts and does not understand the process, he or she tends to bog down a script with a ton of unnecessary dialogue. Thoughts that could take as few as three words are written as three lines. Things that will be apparent on screen are spelled out by characters. I suggest that you watch a bunch of shows and see how quickly the characters get to the point. Just like I believe it is foolish for a book writer not to read books, it is twice as foolish for someone to write television scripts without examining how they are written. You can watch shows and go online and find some sample scripts from popular shows to understand the dialogue aspect more.

Also, because you are limited with pages, you should not go into too much detail about the actions that characters perform. Actors and actresses interpret those actions themselves, and/or the director takes care of that during scene blocking and rehearsal. An action in a script should not take up more than two lines in 99 percent of instances.

You must also include transitional scenes like cutting to cars driving down a street, or showing the sun rise, or showing some extras walking along the beach. Rough cuts are exactly that—rough, and they are extremely obvious. Even if you go back and add those in later, make sure you include them or the show will look crazy on-air.

Those are the overall basics of television scriptwriting. I would suggest taking a course at a local festival or reading some books on the topic and, eventually, if you can afford it and are serious about pursuing it as a career, purchase a license for Final Draft. Most scripts are traded back and forth in Final Draft among the writers, producers, and the networks. Movie Magic is also popular but everyone that I have ever dealt with—and I have written and executive produced two series to date—has used Final Draft.

When it comes to actual scripted programming, it becomes more complicated. The first thing that a writer needs to consider is the budget of the show. Most networks break that down per episode contractually, but if you are shooting out locations (filming all of the scenes that occur within the same space over the entire season instead of moving back and forth)—which I do—the entire budget becomes more important. Backtracking for a second, most reality shows are filmed by episode and the editing turnaround is much faster than scripted programming. With scripted programming, pre-production and post-production take months.

Location, Location, Location

Once you have your budget, you need to determine what is realistic. The first thing that I do is come up with a "location bucket," which is a list of places that I want to utilize within the series, none of which are so extravagant that they will eat up the budget. After I have my location bucket, I remain cognizant of the amount of effort it takes to move tons of people and equipment from one area to another at the location. I break the locations down into two to three areas. Let me make up an example.

There is a show called *The Baseball Life* about a high school baseball team that is trying to make it to the state finals, no matter what the costs. The main character is Ben and his best friend's name is Jerry. My location bucket would look something like this initially (it can always be expanded or trimmed once I get into the actual scriptwriting):

High school interior: hallway, classroom (can be used
    for different teachers if needed), and cafeteria

High school exterior: parking lot, baseball field,
  courtyard
Ben's house: his bedroom, kitchen, basement den
Jerry's house: his bedroom, living room, garage
Fast food restaurant: exterior and interior
Movie theater: exterior and lobby
Open-air shopping center

This would be my starting location bucket. Notice that I choose certain locations within a location that could be the most versatile in setting up different scenes. The hallway of the high school is a great place to have a lot of conversations, shows a lot of drama, and establishes the fact that it is indeed a larger-scale school by allowing you to show a lot of extras. The classroom can easily be changed around to be a math, English, or science room with minor set design choices. The cafeteria is also where a lot of action occurs in a high school. Unless you have a lot of time and a bigger budget, it makes no sense to stage one scene in the principal's office or one scene in the janitorial closet. Not to mention the difficulty of shooting in such a cramped space when it is not necessary. If I had to add one more interior location, it would be the boy's locker room.

We need a baseball field because the show is about baseball. The parking lot of a high school has a lot of activity as kids come and leave, and there should be scenes with the characters arriving and addressing one another or taking off after school. It also gives us the chance to express different things about their characters, like the kinds of cars they drive, whether or not they ride the bus or their bicycles to school, etc. The courtyard could be used as a gathering area for them during all parts of the day, including possibly Ben walking through it at dusk holding his girlfriend's hand and engaged in a deep conversation about them having to go separate ways once they leave for college.

For Ben's house, we need the bedroom since most teens spend most of their time there. The kitchen was chosen because it is a great place for him to interact with his parents. Since he is the main character, parental interaction definitely has to be shown. The basement den could be an interesting "man cave" for Ben and his friends to congregate and play videogames and discuss the season.

I added different rooms for Jerry's house to make it look diverse, with the exception of his bedroom: self-explanatory. The living room is the place where Jerry can interact with his parents and the garage could showcase a hobby that he might share with his father, or we can show him sneaking in after curfew and hanging out with Ben and other friends.

I added a fast food restaurant and movie theater because the show is about teens in a small town and those are the two things they do the most. The open-air shopping center allows us to be able to introduce other townspeople without them having to be at the school or visiting someone's home. Maybe there is a senior citizen store owner that Ben stops by to see often; he or she could even be a grandparent.

The most important thing to keep in mind when picking

out locations is knowing that you should use each one of those locations at least five times over the course of the season, and the houses and school every episode. If you cannot wrap your head around that, you may need to rethink your list. It is easiest to shoot out locations so if you have five scenes on the baseball field, they can all be done in the same day. You shoot them in the order of time of day. If one takes place at sunrise, two take place in the middle of the day, one takes place at dusk, and one takes place at night, that is how they should be shot.

Now that you have your location bucket and your bible, you can begin the writing process. With television shows, three things are crucial to keep in mind: the demographics of the network, the airing time of the show, and the fact that your show will be pitted against hundreds of shows on other channels. It is important to understand the demographics of the network. If your show will not appeal to their audience, you are dead in the water. Then again, they will not likely pick your show up in the first place. Even if they do pick it up, you cannot go off in another direction and expect them to approve the scripts. That is not going to happen. While there can be some creative freedom in television, ultimately all those involved in decision-making for the network have a say in what makes it on air.

The air time of your show is important because it determines how much you can push the envelope, or whether you can push it at all. Certain things will not be aired before a particular time, so a show airing at eight o'clock has to be tamer than a show airing at ten or eleven o'clock. You will know this in advance as well but you must keep it in mind while writing scripts.

Lastly, and most importantly, there is a ton of competition on television. Networks that had big ratings in particular time slots even last year are having major issues this year. With the emergence and growth of Netflix and Hulu, and the ability to watch practically anything on demand, it will only get worse. It is time for television writers to step up their game or face extinction. At this point, writers need to start considering how what they are writing can go viral so people will be encouraged to post, tweet, and discuss the show with online viewing parties. That means your show has to spark them into those actions, so keep that in mind.

Writing Films

Writing films is a little different from writing for television, but not by much. You still have all of the same concerns, especially if it is a made-for-TV film. The one advantage of writing a feature film that will be shown in theaters is that you have more time. Therefore, you can take a little longer—not much longer, though—to set things up.

I simply cannot stand leaving a theater and feeling like I could have seen the same movie on Lifetime or ABC Family. I want movie-going to be an experience. With that said, the ability to do that can be somewhat limited by financing, unless you have a huge budget, but that is not going to happen right off the bat. Even with an extremely low budget, you can still do some amazing things. You will not be able to have car chases, or blow up buildings, but you can still be imaginative enough to make it work.

In addition to all of the things mentioned when I was discussing writing for television, such as the location bucket, for a full-length screenplay I highly recommend using index cards to break down your scenes. Again, you cannot have long, drawn-out scenes. You have to split them up. Instead of twelve to eighteen scenes, for a feature you could be talking eighty to one hundred easily, with the splits between the various scenarios and transitional scenes. Final Draft actually has index cards included in the software, but regular index cards from the grocery store will do. A script should be between ninety and one hundred pages but it varies and depends highly on the budget. The more pages, the longer the production, the more the expenses, and the longer the time it takes for post-production. Each scene should contribute to the progress of the plot or the development of the characters. If it does not, it needs to go down into your memory bank as a good thought but not a practical one.

Most screenplays are written in three acts. More experienced writers freestyle, but as a beginner I suggest you study and use that method.

The best way for me to describe it is this: The first act is the set-up. It introduces the characters and the situation and guides us into the main body / conflict of the story. The action is ascending and the first plot is clearly introduced, signifying the end of act one. The second act is the confrontation. This is where most of the action happens and where the drama and tension rises. It is longer than the first act. At the end of act two, the second plot is introduced (you should always have a red herring that comes out of nowhere so viewers will be on the edge of their seats). The third act is the resolution. The action starts to die down, things start returning to normal, and all is good with the world. Of course, you can always hit viewers with a shocker at the end, sparking speculation that there will be a sequel or simply to scare them to death on the ride home. Of course, these details depend on the genre of the script, but the overall premise is the same.

For a one hundred–page script, I would break it down into something like this:

Act One: twenty-five pages
Act Two: sixty pages
Act Three: fifteen pages

None of that is exact but it is a good guideline to begin with. There are many diagrams and hundreds of sample scripts readily available online that you can read for more clarification. However, the best way to understand the pace of scripts is to watch movies and try to determine where the acts switch over and where the plots are introduced.

The film has to be exciting enough to edit some clips into

an amazing trailer that will make people flock to the theater. We all realize that there have been many movies that have fallen way short of their trailers, or every key moment in the film was in the trailer. You need to aspire for more.

The Bottom Line

No matter which medium you choose to write in, or if you choose to write in all four—which I have done and will continue to do—the important thing is to have overall mass appeal. The more people that can relate to your works, the better. Even if there is a sentimental point that you are trying to get across, you need to be able to expand that to affect the most people. In all of this, it should be about having fun. Putting too much pressure on yourself will backfire every time. Do not jump out and proclaim that you can do something that you cannot do. Even with me, I elected not to write a screenplay when asked because, at the time, I did not feel comfortable doing it. Now, it is a breeze. I regret not doing it from the beginning but such is life, and opportunities abound to write many, many more.

I enjoy writing in all media. Each one presents its own challenges and rewards. At some point, I would recommend at least testing the waters in each. There is nothing wrong with expanding your horizons and gaining knowledge and experience in various areas.

Most people will never understand the complexity of

pulling off even one breathtaking movie scene. How many different people and things have to come together in perfect unison to make it seem authentic. I did one fight scene on *Zane's The Jump Off* and it took half the day, required a stuntman on set to instruct the actors, and all of that work had to go into what ended up being less than twenty seconds on screen. So when I see movie franchises like *Superman*, *Spiderman*, and *Iron Man*, I tense up at the very thought of having to pull some of those scenes off. It takes hundreds of people, sometimes thousands of people, coming together in unison to make it work. Ultimately, the director is responsible for making it "speak to the audience." When you think of a director, many believe they sit there eating a turkey sandwich on rye in a cozy chair and yell "action" after everything is in place. That could not be further from the truth. A director has to begin working on a film months before the first camera is set up and spends hours upon hours a day setting up shot lists, organizing camera setups—dozens, sometimes hundreds in a day—and making sure that all of the coverage necessary is obtained. You can do some pick-up shots but you cannot go back and re-create a two- or three-million-dollar-per-day set with hundreds or thousands of extras on a whim if you forget to do something.

While it is true that some people have it easier than others in the battle of the bulge, those with 6 percent body fat, eight-pack abs, and incredibly toned bodies work at them. You can be skinny and out of shape and you can be larger and in amazing health. A lot of people complain about their weight and say that it is not fair that so-and-so looks so good, but so-and-so is at the gym at least five times a week, or running several miles a day, or doing exercise DVDs at home, or attending local Zumba classes at the community center. So-and-so is swimming three times a week, not eating after seven in the evening, not eating sweet and white potatoes, bread, and rice, and getting the appropriate amount of sleep at night. So-and-so definitely slips up every now and then and skips a workout or eats a slice of that lemon cake, but they make up for it later. And it is not about what others see them doing; it is about what they see themselves doing.

When it comes to writing, it is a profession that definitely is not accomplished by being concerned about what people see you doing. Sure, you can join a writers group—a great idea for many—or get a writing partner who holds you accountable for a certain amount of words to be written daily. But ultimately, failure or success to complete a novel, script, or nonfiction book is wedged on your shoulders. You have to do whatever it takes to accomplish the goal, even if you have to do it in baby steps. Establish a routine that is reasonable for your lifestyle and stick to it, even when you are traveling or out of your normal comfort zone. There are many times when I am on tour and people ask me out to dinner after a lecture or signing, or at a writing conference where the majority of the writers hang out at the bars and go clubbing. There are times when I am on Zane-branded destination trips and people want me to hang out with them outside of the scheduled events. My response is always the same: I need to go back to my room and work. It is not that I am being antisocial, or that I do not enjoy their company. It is because I have a commitment to myself to complete a task that I have in mind.

I lost count long ago of comments regarding how lucky I am to have sold millions of books, written so many books, published so many books, written and executive produced television series, to have my books turned into major films, and so on and so on. I lost count of the other authors stating that they are going to start an imprint, or implying that they deserve an imprint like me because they are famous. Most would not want to, or could not, handle the level of work that I have to put in on a daily basis. They do not see the late-night, bicoastal conference calls, the fourteen to sixteen hours per day I put in on a film set, the workload of having to churn out scripts and books at the same time, the effort I put forth to make sure that the sixty books that I publish per year are all in top-notch shape. They do not have to deal with more than a hundred authors on their slate, production, publicity, sales, marketing, and editorial departments. They do not have to deal with a couple dozen cast members and seventy-five plus crew members and be responsible for six figures a day being spent wisely.

My relatives and friends see how hard I work. One of my cousins stayed with me last year and after one week, she was stressing out over my schedule and it was not even her schedule. She realized that I do not sit on the sofa at night eating bon-bons and watching women bully each other or fight over trifling men on reality shows. Outside of spending quality time with my family, I am working at night. The kids have been asleep for hours and I am still up, sitting at one of the various desktops or laptops I have scattered around the house—so one is near when something hits me—trying to accomplish one of my goals.

A successful writing career is not going to fall into your lap. I have to be content with my content and believe that it will be impactful on someone's life before I let it go.

Establish your disciplinary path and stick to it. Stop talking about writing your masterpiece and actually do it. Do not sit back and act in awe at what someone else is doing with their talent. Instead, use your talent and imagination. But let me leave this chapter with one word of caution: do not let your head become consumed with how much money can be made from your words. Be concerned about how many hearts you can touch.

CHAPTER 8

The Editorial Process

If you have finished a manuscript, then it is time to go into the editorial process. Hopefully, you have been editing your book all along and have gone back and read your work at least once after completing each chapter. I say "hopefully" in a sarcastic way. In my opinion, and based on the thousands of manuscripts that I read, edit, or even glance through, that is sadly not the case. I might make a lot of people upset with this chapter but I am going to let it all out. It is absolutely ridiculous for anyone to assume that they can throw together a book and then expect other people to actually do "the real writing."

I have seen discussions on social networks regarding the responsibilities of an editor. Many people have declared that the editor is the one who is supposed to "fix the book." Some say, "I'm a writer, not an editor." Again, ridiculous. If you are one of those who actually believes that, you need to go ahead and put my book down now. You are not worthy of reading a serious book on writing and publishing. You are treating the industry that I love like a joke and I do not appreciate it. I do not care if you have a third-grade education, recently got released from a twenty-year prison sentence, have twelve kids, and barely enough time to even write, or have four full-time jobs, there is no excuse for sending a sloppy book to anyone.

Certain writers get upset when their genre is not taken seriously and has a bad reputation. It is not based on the implications of the storylines: gang-banging, drugs, murder, etc. I have read, and published, excellent "street novels." It is based on the monumental mistakes made throughout the books that were not properly edited. I recently edited a book that had more than thirteen thousand mistakes. Yes, I said thirteen thousand mistakes. I took on that task because the manuscript was overdue and it was what had to be done. After looking through the first chapter, I was too embarrassed to send it out to a freelance editor, and I did not even write it. Plus, I realized that I was a faster editor and time was of the essence. Someone else would have completely lost it if presented with the project and, quite frankly, no amount of money would have been worth enduring the pain. It took at least ten thousand dollars worth of my own time to edit it. As the publisher of the book, I was not compensated. Then my publishing director had to go through the book again and find the numerous mistakes that I missed because I was practically brain dead after I finished. You have to be able to write if you want to be a writer.

I am not saying that editors should not work and earn their pay. What I am saying is that the quality and overall professional level of a book begins and ends with the original writer. If a book needs to be edited three or four times— one author told me that he has six editors—then there is a serious issue. All of this is to say, before you send your book to an editor or submit it to your publisher, read the book. In Microsoft Word, the software will point out half of the mistakes to you with red or green lines under the words. Some people are too lazy to even do that. It does come down to laziness—either that or arrogance.

If you think you are too cute to go on Google and double-check the proper names of people, places, or things, you need to find another profession. If you think your words are so amazing that you could not have possibly written a "hot mess" of a manuscript, then you are being completely delusional. It is possible for someone to turn in a "clean book" with few errors. A few of my authors do that every single time. Reading their books is like a breath of fresh air in a seven hundred–acre forest fire. I appreciate their effort, whether it means that they actually understand correct grammar or they had someone else read it before presenting it to me.

The most important thing in selecting an editor is making sure that they can actually edit. We have used dozens of freelance editors throughout the years and it is always a struggle to find one that is actually qualified. We have had famous authors, employees at major publishing houses, college English professors, and other top-notch professionals who did horrific editing. We have paid to have books edited and then had to edit them all over again in-house. Please do not allow Becky down the street who has a 4.0 at the local university to edit your book unless she actually does it on the regular. Do not allow your polished aunt in Savannah, Georgia, to edit your book. If someone advertises as an editor, make them take a test with one of your chapters before you hire them for the entire project. You would not believe the number of people running editing companies who cannot edit. You need to make sure that you are hiring someone who knows what they are doing and someone who can do it in a timely fashion, especially when you are working against strong deadlines from a publisher.

There are several different types of editing. I will go over each one for you in this chapter.

Basic Proofreading

Basic proofreading is best utilized by those writers who are confident in their writing and only need someone to check their spelling, grammar, punctuation, and subject-verb agreement. They have double-checked all of the pertinent information themselves and understand proper English. Even when someone is extremely good in English, they should still have someone else go behind them to make sure.

Reduction Editing

Some writers have an issue with being too wordy and adding in way too much information in their books, no matter what the genre. Some write books so long that they often have to cut the books into two. A reduction editor goes through a manuscript and deletes, truncates, and omits unnecessary and excess language without losing any of the pertinent information or style of the book. If you realize that your book is way too long, this is definitely a skill that your editor should possess.

Standard Editing

Standard editing is comprised of spell-checking, grammar, punctuation, transitional phrasing, continuity, flowing of thoughts, support of statements (fact-checking), and consistency and appropriateness of verb tenses. This is for someone who has some confidence in their writing but realizes that they probably overlooked quite a few things.

Technical Editing

Technical editing is standard editing on steroids. It is all of the elements of standard with the formation of references, citations, and footnotes included. The editor should be an expert in your preferred style. In the literary industry, that is the *Chicago Manual of Style*. Others include The Modern Language Association's *MLA Style Manual* and the American Psychological Association's APA style that has a set of standards of its own. MLA is adopted by most colleges and universities as a scholarly style and APA is used mostly for the social sciences. Depending on the topic of your book, one of these should pertain to it.

Content Editor

Content editing includes standard and technical editing but the editor will also make plot and character development suggestions. Obviously, this type of editor should have some type of creative imagination themselves. Otherwise, they would really have nothing to offer. This is not to say that you have to accept whatever they suggest as the gospel. It is up to you to decide whether or not you feel it will improve your book. However, once you hire them to do content editing, do not get offended if they truly pick your book apart. We have used some good content editors who have sent pages and pages of queries in regards to the books. That could mean anything from the characters not being appealing enough to holes in the storyline to timelines being way off. For inexperienced writers, I would highly suggest getting a content editor. It is more than a simple notion to write a book.

Extreme Content Editing

People might call this various things but I call it *extreme*. This type of editing is when you pay someone to do extensive rewrites of your books, something that I have done throughout the years for various authors without compensation. Not anymore. I consider myself in this role as a crutch, and a crutch is supposed to be a temporary thing, not permanent. An extreme editor will end up rewriting up to 50 percent of your book. That actually makes them your coauthor. If you need this type of editorial help, I would suggest giving up on writing altogether. The only time that this might be acceptable—in my opinion—is in the case of a celebrity or entrepreneur or someone who feels like they have a compelling story and they use a ghostwriter. In that case, it is expected that the writer will need a lot of work. Outside of that, if you want to become a writer, grow yourself into a writer.

One of the best ways to catch a lot of your mistakes within a manuscript is to read it out loud to yourself, slowly and carefully. When we read, especially something that we wrote and already know what comes next, our mind tends to skip over the obvious. If you read a sentence out loud and a word like *a* or *and* is missing, it is obvious.

Another good idea is to finish a book and set the manuscript aside for a month or two, if time allows, and then reread it with fresh eyes. That is good for a couple of reasons. First, the glaring mistakes will be more apparent. Secondly, you will not be as caught up in the characters and storyline as you were when you were writing. You can then catch some of the possible flaws in the story and see how it can be improved.

If you have a deadline to turn your book in to the publisher, usually one that is several months away or more, try to finish the book at least two months before that deadline. That allows you enough time to go through an editing process before you turn it in. Some of you are thinking that is what the editors at the publishing houses are for. To some degree, that is true, but your manuscript has to be accepted by the publisher and they might kick it back if they find it to be mediocre at best. Even if they accept it, in the back of their minds they are thinking that there are plenty of other writers out there begging for an opportunity who take the craft more seriously. That is a constant discussion within our imprint, as we have hundreds of good submissions on any given day. I have dropped many authors from my slate due to a continuous habit of turning in sloppy manuscripts. I have heard that some other publishers are willing to take on the daunting task of having to edit books over and over and will spend up to eight hours even fixing formatting. That is not acceptable with me and it speaks volumes about a writer's commitment to establishing a long-term career.

The Bottom Line

An editor is not supposed to be your coauthor. They are supposed to go over certain elements of the book but not completely rewrite it to make you appear to have more skills than you actually have. Even if you have a selected few readers, you will not obtain the true level of success that you seek. Eventually, they will discover other writers with much more to offer.

PART 2

PUBLISHING

CHAPTER 9

Writer vs. Author

I often speak on this topic at writers' conferences or during speeches. Even during casual conversations, it often comes up—mostly out of frustration. As a publisher, I cannot be expected to be the sole promoter of someone else's work. Nor can my publicity department be expected to take on the task alone. Now that we have come to the point where you should have a polished and finished product, one that you have painstakingly spent your time, tears, and talent to get out, word for word, you need to realize one important thing: there is a huge difference between being a writer and being an author.

When I write, it is not a group effort; I am not on some specific assignment, and I do not have anyone watching over my shoulder—unless you count my nosey kids. One walked up a moment ago and is leaning on me right this second. Writing is a solitary, introverted process, for the most part. Of course, there are exceptions for people who decide to co-author a book, people who utilize ghostwriters, etc. That is a different story and, even then, there is still a big difference between a writer and an author.

An author is a personality. Many are not prepared, or are ill-prepared, to accept that role. You can pen the best work of the year, worthy of the Pulitzer Prize, but if no one knows about it, it rarely matters. Whether you end up self-publishing or land a deal with a major publisher, you are the best promoter of your work. But it is not actually about engaging people in your work; it is about engaging them in you. Unless there is something appealing about you overall, rarely will people be willing to plunk down their hard-earned money to purchase your book. Not unless you are able to get the word-of-mouth buzz going enough so that your book becomes the latest craze that everyone feels they must read.

Many of my authors are people who I first met in person and I was impressed with their personalities, their conviction, and their passion. Now, granted, some of them introduced me to their representatives right away, so their personalities became clearer later on down the road, but at least something about them got them through the initial door.

If a person is a complete ass, they should not allow that to be seen in person. I have seen such people put on pretenses in public and then transform into demons after the lights dim, but they sold a lot of books. I have seen authors who have nothing but venom in their hearts pull the wool over unsuspecting eyes and sell a lot of books. If the books are good, that is what matters to the readers at that point. But even if a book is poorly written, an author with a bubbly personality can sell out of them. Of course, that ultimately backfires since there are so many outlets for displeased readers to post negative reviews.

I even know of several "authors" who have never written a book but manage to make the *New York Times* bestseller list time and time again—not speculation, but fact. They have built an entire career on being a personality, and to that, I say whatever is clever. While I am sure many readers would be sorely upset if they ever found out, it does not negate the fact that they enjoyed the works.

This will not be a long chapter but it is definitely one that I felt deserved to be separated and highlighted from the rest of the book. It is imperative that whether you are online or in person, you should not rub people the wrong way. That pertains to readers, bookstore employees and managers, other authors, agents, and definitely publishers. As a publisher for fifteen years, and the executive producer of television series and films, I can tell you right now that 99 percent of people are easily replaceable. When it comes to readers, they will read someone else. When it comes to an agent, they will represent someone else. When it comes to publishers, they will publish someone else. It is as simple as that.

If you are shy, it is time for you to emerge from that shell, even if you do it temporarily and go right back in there once an appearance is over. Do not arrive at a book signing and sit there at the table waiting for people to approach you to inquire about your book. Stand up and be proud of what you have written, introduce yourself properly and ask for a moment of their time. Hand them your book so they can scan over the front and back covers. Maintain eye contact with them as you pitch the concept to them. At most book signings, you only have a moment to be convincing. Then they are either handing the book back to you and walking away, possibly with one of your bookmarks, promising to consider purchasing it later or downloading it as an ebook, or they are headed to the register to purchase it so you can sign it for them afterward.

I am going to discuss online marketing and social networking in a later chapter but it is imperative to have a major presence in cyberspace. However, it needs to be a positive one. Too many authors have totally killed their careers by talking trash about their agents, publishers, and other authors on the World Wide Web. They think it is cute at the time and they want to draw attention to themselves. Some want to show their toughness and their "I could not care less what others say, I am amazing!" attitudes. Let me say this: there are no big I's and little U's in the world and even fewer in the publishing industry. If you believe otherwise, you are sadly mistaken.

Humility takes you a long way in life; being egotistical

quickly makes everyone avoid you. The literary industry is a very small, close-knit community, so what you do and say is rarely a secret. If you say something negative about your agent, they will hear about it. If you say something negative about your publisher, they will *definitely* hear about it. If you say something negative about another author, especially one with legions of dedicated readers, they will hear about it. The same goes for booksellers. Many, many bookstores have told me what other authors have said about me. Many, many authors have told me what other authors have said about me—those I know in passing, those that I publish, and some authors that I have never met. It is truly sad and disappointing to see people continually block their blessings.

Never think that you are bigger than your publisher. Never talk down to your publisher or anyone who works for them. You will quickly find yourself seeking another offer elsewhere, and guess what happens? The other publishers will wonder why you are no longer being published by the first house. Trying to spin a negative theory about your previous publisher is the kiss of death, especially if you complain about lack of publicity and marketing, or say that you did not get a big enough advance. Publishers will think that you will also ultimately talk about them similarly.

That relates to any career. Prior to "becoming Zane," I was in corporate America and witnessed it time and time again. I was working in an office with a young man who had a problem with women in positions of authority. He finally came out and admitted that. It was an industry made up of "the good ol' boy network," and a lot of the men took issue with women. It was okay for him to feel that way, but he went too far when he called me into the conference room one day to try to correct me. First of all, he had no business calling me into anyplace to discuss anything in that tone, and secondly, he was not even correct in what he was saying. I pointed out to him that the paperwork he presented to me was not even signed by me—in fact, I had never seen it—and then laughed my way out of the room to my next appointment. One of the other men on the team told me that he had warned the young man not to call me in there. He said that the other one had even asked him if "he wanted a piece of the action."

Then he really went and did it. After the regional manager, also a female, and the person he should have approached if he felt he had an issue with me, called him on the carpet and told him to never say another negative word to me, he ran off to one of our clients and asked for a position with their corporation, stating a bunch of negative things about her. Of course, the CEO of our client corporation went right back and told her what was said later that week during a lunch meeting. That was the beginning of the end for my coworker at that company. He went from making nearly two hundred thousand a year to working at the desk of a rental car company. It can happen in the publishing world in the same way. Keep that in mind.

The Bottom Line

You have to possess thick skin to be an author. Again, writing is done in solitude, but once you become published, it is a different situation. Even when you are seeking a deal, you have to be careful what you say and how you say it. If you get an agent or a deal, you cannot go on the defensive when anyone—agent, editor, or publisher—makes suggestions to improve your work. Some authors have become downright combative with me over their material.

If you get negative reviews, you cannot go on the defensive. People are entitled to their opinion and I have never seen a single author that got all positive reviews from everyone under the sun. Too many authors get caught up in their emotions and it is understandable to an extent. Hopefully, you have given it your all and put all of your sweat and tears into the book, but that does not mean the entire world will appreciate it. I often get asked how I deal with criticism and my response is always the same: I do not deal with it. I am satisfied with my work long before I present it to the public eye. People may love me or hate me, but they will remember me. Most of my criticism comes from people who have not even read my books or watched my shows or films in the first place. A lot of it comes from other authors who resent the fact that I have been able to obtain more attention and success than they have. Nothing excites me more than to see other authors succeed and make waves in the industry. I find it inspiring, not stifling.

I am not the most outgoing person around strangers. With people that I know, I will open up and talk to them for hours, but in large groups I would rather observe. For that reason, I was initially reluctant to do book signings when I finally decided to reveal myself four years after my first book and go on "The Zane Love Bus Tour." My apprehension stemmed from not wanting attendees to think that I was stuck up, something that could not be any further from the case. I had to get over that and it all turned out fine. Those of you who have met me know that I am extremely down to earth. All of that is to say that I practice what I preach.

You cannot expect people to rush up to you, begging to buy your book as an up-and-coming author. One year, my imprint was participating in the Baltimore Book Festival—a three-day event. The first night, I came out there and saw all of my authors sitting behind the tables like prima donnas waiting for people to approach them. By morning, the tent was completely rearranged, the tables were pushed to the back, and all chairs had been removed. When we do conventions and fairs, I spend most of my time observing and then have staff meetings and go down the list of authors, one by one, and ask my staff if they would have purchased a book from any of them if they were a book browser—and why or why not? I can tell you unequivocally that the authors who sell the most books at events are the ones who engage the audience. The ones who sell the most books overall are the ones who are social butterflies on Facebook and Twitter. They are the ones who visit book clubs—both locally and nationally—and always promote themselves with bookmarks, T-shirts, or book giveaways. And they can do it consistently, book after book after book. The good reading material is part of it—I have never published a mediocre book—but the longevity is from the fact that readers adore them, book clubs want to support them, and bookstore managers are delighted to have them return. On the flip side, there are certain authors who bookstores will not entertain holding a signing for, even if it means losing out on a lot of sales.

Some of the demands that authors make for a book signing or appearance are ridiculous. I am often asked what I need, and all I say is a good supply of pens and a bottle of water or a diet soda. That's it. No fruit platters, frozen grapes, specialty tablecloths or chairs, particular pens, or anything in between. I am there to appreciate the people who A) appreciated me enough to have me and B) appreciated me enough to make a special trip to meet me. Even if the library or bookstore tries to tell people that they have to wait until all books are signed before I will take photos, or that I will only sign the new book, I never go along with that plan. If someone purchased thirty of my books and they have them in two duffle bags and want me to sign them all, that is exactly what I am going to do. I am going to make an attempt to have some type of conversation, albeit brief, with each person. Some authors will not even personalize a book. I find that to be ridiculous. I am going to show my fans the love and attention that they deserve, to the best of my ability. I take nothing for granted, even at this stage in my career.

So for all of you shy ones, stuck-up ones, stressed-out ones, etc., you need to get over all of that. Not now, but *right now*. If you are nervous about doing a reading, practice, practice, practice. If you do not believe you can take a negative review in stride, do not read your reviews at all. If you feel the need to vent and say something negative about any of your counterparts, or professional associates, put it in a journal. Stop looking for cosigners. It will backfire and they will still be with the agent or publisher when you are wondering why no one wants to be bothered with you any longer. You could fill up an entire graveyard with writers who have killed their own careers—talented writers at that—because they could not control their mouths or their emotions.

CHAPTER 10

Literary Agents

If you desire to land a deal with major/traditional publishers, and unless you have a direct route into one, you will need to hire a literary agent first. Of course, there are exceptions, e.g. if you are "discovered," as I was. It may seem unfair that you cannot simply print out your ninety thousand–word manuscript, ship it via courier to Avenue of the Americas in New York City, and receive a phone call a week later from a zealous editor who wants to sign you up. But put yourself in their place: How many books could you read a week, even if it was your job?

Literary agents serve a purpose for writers and publishers. They are the first line of defense for publishers. They choose among the projects most likely to do well in the marketplace and for the particular editors and publishers. They save time for publishers who are not only busy looking out for the next best project but also with projects already under contract and in production—hundreds of titles a year in the case of major publishers. In my imprint alone, we have published up to eight books per month, and we are but one of dozens of imprints at Simon & Schuster. An agent or agency can have such an established connection and reputation with publishers that their clients will be considered based solely on their representation and recommendation.

In any case, patience is required. Do not expect a miracle within the first few weeks and a phone call from your agent with five deals for you to select from. In fact, it could take months or even years to get a deal. Trust that the agent is just as frustrated as you. At a certain point, one or both of you may wish to part ways if you don't make progress within a reasonable amount of time. It does not mean that the agent does not believe in you. Any reputable agent would never take you on as a client if that were the case. It might simply mean that no publisher envisions successfully publishing the work.

There are many important factors in identifying the appropriate agent for you. Most agents tend toward particular niches, markets, and genres. Realize that, with open solicitation, 99 percent of what they receive will not fit. They often find enough appropriate clients by word-of-mouth from their current clients.

It is like a butterfly effect. Agents prefer that authors they respect recommend manuscripts, and publishers prefer that agents they respect recommend the same. Over the years, I have recommended at least a couple dozen authors to my agent, and with the exception of a couple, she chose to represent them all. Some are bestselling authors with dozens of titles themselves at this point. Some of them I met while I was out and about, and others approached me via email or snail mail. Some simply fell into my inner circle.

On the flip side, because I respect my agent and know what kinds of books she tends to represent, I am open to taking a look at whatever she sends to me for Strebor. Over the years, I have acquired dozens of titles from her roster of authors, and there have been very few that have not piqued my interest. Now she also has tons of material that she knows does not fit the bill with me so she does not send it. She submits it to the various other acquisitions editors at publishing houses. That is one trait that makes someone a good agent.

None of this means that you cannot approach an agent directly—not at all. Agents get tons of clients that way. You may get a lot of rejection letters. Do not automatically take that to mean that you are not a good writer. The agent may not represent that genre, they may already have too many authors in that genre, they may be overwhelmed with work, or they may have decided, based on a mediocre query letter or synopsis, that you are not of any interest to them.

That brings me to my next point: the query letter. A query letter should be a formal letter proposing your writing ideas and giving a snippet of why you should be considered as a client. In my opinion, it should be somewhere between four hundred and a thousand words. Any more or less can be a turnoff. An extremely short one means that you do not feel like you have to impress anyone, that you are that dude or chick and the world should already know it. It does not express enough about you or your work for anyone to gauge something of value. One of too great a length prevents the agent from getting to the enclosed synopsis and sample chapters that should also be included. Some suggest only sending a query letter. As a publisher, I can tell you that I have rarely requested a manuscript based solely on a query letter. I will explain that further in a moment.

A query letter should include four major things:

1. the topic of the work,

2. the target audience of the work,

3. a short description of the plot,

4. a brief bio of the author.

Do not let the bio part scare you. Be honest, because there is no requirement to have a Master's in English to write a book, or to have been previously published in six different languages. If you are a waitress, say that. If you are a day care provider, say that. If you are currently incarcerated, say that. The bio should simply explain what makes you interesting. So explain a little about where you are from, what you do, and what inspires you to write. If your book is a memoir, explain what motivated you to write it. Keep it short but engaging and leave it at that.

The query is your first impression to an agent or a publisher. I have had people misspell my name as Zhane instead of Zane, or misspell Strebor Books as Straybor Books. Just like you would take the time to double-check the proper names of a corporation where you are applying for a job before submitting a cover letter with your resume, it is imperative that you do the same with an agent. To make such a careless mistake tells the agent a couple of things: A) you are probably sending query letters to numerous agents and rushing through the process and B) you are not concerned about editing your work. I discussed that at length in the chapter on editing.

Next up should be the synopsis, or synopses if you are submitting more than one title for review. If you have more than one completed manuscript, send them for both. If you have a lot of completed manuscripts, select the two that you consider to be the best representation of your writing style and note that you have several more. That is a good look because it tells an agent that you will probably not be a "one-off" author. Most agents prefer to establish career authors; that way their initial efforts can continue to pay off for many years.

The synopsis should be entertaining, detailed, and expressive. Let's face it: most story concepts have been written in some fashion before. But your spin on the story should be different; that's the key to success. So whether it is a story of overcoming adversity, abuse, or discrimination, or a story of infidelity, heartbreak, or reigniting the flames in a relationship, or a story of murder, mayhem, or mystery, you need to express why your work is different and compelling. There have been many times when I have read a query letter and thought to myself, *Oh, another story about a female stressing over not finding a husband by a certain age after a string of failed relationships!* Then, after reading the synopsis, I am either not impressed because it sounds like the same old thing, or I am anxious to read the sample chapters because the description was so fascinating.

If the mere thought of writing a synopsis seems more frightening of a concept than writing an actual book, I have a couple of suggestions. Read the copy of existing books and descriptions of books in publisher catalogues and/or on websites. Look at how professional copywriters do it. When I first read the copy my publisher used for my novel *Addicted*, which I had previously self-published, it got me excited to "read" the novel—and I'm the one who wrote it. You can learn a tremendous amount by studying what has worked for others. Also, you could record yourself describing the book and then pull out key elements from listening to it over and over. Or ask a friend or relative to listen to it and tell you what sparks their interest the most.

After you have crafted a crisp, straight-to-the-key-points query letter and have polished your synopsis—one that has been properly edited—you'll need two or three sample chapters to really make an impact on an agent.

Whatever you do, *do not* send random chapters that you

think are the better parts of your book. Huge mistake for a couple of reasons. First, the book needs to be engaging from page one, and if you send chapter twelve, sixteen, and thirty, that is a red flag. So what if those chapters are incredible? Readers will put your book down way before chapter twelve if the beginning does not draw them in. There have been many books that I heard were amazing via word-of-mouth, and I had to put them down after the first few chapters because I was about to fall asleep. A few of them I did eventually go back to and complete and was pleasantly surprised that they got much better. But your writing should not feel like a chore for a reader or an agent.

Secondly, it is hard for an agent to gauge your ability to let a storyline flow by reading nonconsecutive chapters. That is like turning on a made-for-TV movie halfway through the first act, going to put on dinner, catching a snippet of act two, and then talking on the phone for another thirty minutes and then catching the ending. You might say to yourself that it looked interesting but it was hard to tell because you did not see the beginning. Send consecutive chapters from the beginning of the book. If you are a strong writer, that will be apparent right away and not based solely on the climactic, pivotal points of the storyline.

Following the steps that I laid out does not guarantee that you will land an agent. Sometimes it takes time and sometimes it does not happen at all. But many authors have gone on to be at the top of the writing game after receiving dozens of rejection letters from agents. I had one agent apologize to me more than a decade later and added that allowing me to slip through her fingers was the most stupid mistake she had ever made. Now she has found herself in the position of trying to sell books to me, a person that she at first deemed not good enough to represent. All of that is to say that you should remain steadfast and determined when it comes to your dreams. Even if you never find an agent, it does not mean that you cannot have a successful career. It only means that you will have to find another way to achieve what you desire. Being completely cliché: it is true that winners never quit and quitters never win.

The Role of an Agent

Now that we have discussed how to approach an agent, let us consider what you should do once you have one or more interested in representing you. What is next? First, you need to ask them for references. Yes, references. Granted, you should realize they did not have to even consider you as a client, but the level of comfort should work both ways. Unless you were referred to the agent and have studied their track record, you have every right to inquire about other authors they represent and how many books they have sold over the previous twenty-four months. I use that as a timeframe because not all agents remain tied into publishers forever. Many burn their bridges over time by making too many unrealistic demands, having a poor attitude, or not following through. Therefore, it is imperative that you find out what they have done as of late.

There are some agents whom I have purchased books from in the past that I would not purchase from ever again and others whom I am delighted to work with. They are timely in getting back to me with any required information and seem sincerely concerned about the welfare of their authors. The ones who have turned me off completely are ones who are obviously inexperienced, incompetent, over-reaching, and out to make a fast buck. They have managed to convince unsuspecting people that they are capable of making all of their dreams come true. Any agent that portrays an unrealistic view of the publishing climate is not a good agent. An upside of the Internet is that you can do a quick web search and find out information about them, based on the thoughts of various individuals. Not seeing anything at all is also a red flag, by the way. Anyone who has had any type of impact in publishing would have some kind of Internet presence, even if it's only in articles, acknowledgments by their clients, or some kind of biographical sketch.

I am not implying that new agents do not deserve an opportunity to get clients. However, they need to have some sort of background in the industry, either as a writer, editor, publisher, or something that would provide them the in-roads and respect to get your work through the door. Publishers receiving material from an agent they have never heard of is only a minor step up from trying to send it in yourself. They do not know any more about your agent than they do about you. Most agents have a background with a publishing house, but if you go with an author—past or present—as your agent, make sure that they have a proven track record with their own body of work.

I have personally seen authors who have not sold even ten thousand books over the course of their entire careers suddenly become agents and try to direct others on how to become successful. Some of them cannot even get another publishing deal themselves but manage to convince other writers that they have their foot in the door. Then there are authors with long, proven track records, ones that are highly respected in the industry, who become agents. I have purchased books from them numerous times. I have considered publishing books from some of the ones who cannot get a deal themselves, but they generally mess up the deal by giving poor advice or making unrealistic demands. An agent can truly make or break a career so you need to make sure that whoever you go with has the expertise, demeanor, and overall ability to represent you in the most positive light.

A good agent is not one who simply collects 10 to 20 percent of your advances and royalties. A good agent is a coach, a cheerleader, and a campaigner for you. He or she is not a miracle worker and you should not expect instantaneous success. They will take the time out to read, lightly edit, and critique your work. They will not send out a raggedy version of your book, only for it to be rejected. As bad as it is for me as a publisher to receive a book with errors on every other page from a writer, it is ten times as bad to receive one from an agent. Agents out for a quick dollar will let the book slip through their fingertips and submit it exactly like you submitted it to them. A good agent will go over it, make suggestions and corrections, and encourage you to improve upon it if needed. I am not saying that an agent should copyedit an entire book. What I am saying is that they should read it and not let blatant storyline issues and extensive grammatical errors land on any acquisition editor's desk. It makes no sense because a rejection of your work is also a rejection of their work, and a waste of time and effort for you both.

If you are like most authors and dream of one day seeing your work on the big screen, you should also inquire about that agent's connections in the theatrical space. Even though most do not do that sort of work full-time, reputable agents have forged associations over time with producers, entertainment attorneys, and the larger talent agencies in Los Angeles. All of the major agencies in California have agents dedicated to packaging and developing projects based on books. Truth be told, most movies are based on books. That said, the competition is even thicker in Hollywood. While a large publishing house may publish a few thousand books across all genres yearly, for movie studios the number of works produced is about 2 to 5 percent of that and about half a percent of that for networks. For that reason, you should try to hire an agent who has coagent partnerships with various people in the industry.

Communication with your agent should be mutual, and even if you do not reach them immediately they should get back to you in a timely fashion. Keep in mind that you are not their only client and that they cannot spend too much time holding your hand. Their time would rather be spent trying to make things happen for you. For the most part, they should inform you of what they are doing on your behalf but they may not tell you everything for fear of getting your hopes up. I often submit scripts and books of my authors to people in Hollywood without telling them about it. Better not to get people's hopes up unnecessarily.

Whatever you do, please do not go diva on your agent. Yes, you are allowing them to represent you, but they are also allowing you to be their client. Most agents are already established in the industry and have had many authors come and go from their lives. Cutting you off might not be the end of the world to them, but it could very well be the end of the line for you. If you know that you are not a patient person, if you tend to have a negative attitude, if you are constantly rubbing people the wrong way, you may not be walking the road with your agent for very long. Most have a very low tolerance for people speaking down to them, and making accusations that they are not doing enough for you will get you nowhere.

The Bottom Line

How you structure a contract with an agent is up to you, but I would not sign away the farm. It should be for a limited time period, with renewable options as long as all is well, and include an out-clause for either party if the situation is not working. They should not have an ongoing right to your work into perpetuity or any right to future work that you write if the relationship is terminated. It should not state that if you sign with any of the publishers that they submitted your work to within the next several years they still get a percentage. It could be that the publisher was feeling you but not feeling them and will offer you a deal outside of their involvement. It could mean that the first time it was submitted it did not fit the bill of what they were looking for at the time. It could mean that they did not have the time to actually consider your work the first time around. As a publisher, I have had all three of those scenarios happen. On the flip side, I have offered people deals that they accepted, only to turn around and acquire an agent who then steps in and overreaches to the point where I have to rescind the offer.

Do not sign with an agent out of desperation. Do not sign with an agent whom you have never heard of, or one who does not have a bona fide track record that you can verify. Do not sign with an agent who has no references, or refuses to allow you to contact their other clients. Do not sign with an agent who you believe is money hungry and one that might blow a deal for you, move on, and leave you and your manuscript flapping in the wind after they have burned a bunch of bridges at publishing houses with your name attached. Do not sign with an agent who wants you to pay them out-of-pocket for them to represent you. Do not agree to give an agent more than 20 percent of your earned monies.

Do your research and take your time determining which

agents fit your writing style. Do look inside the books of authors you admire, read their acknowledgments and see who their agents are. Do approach some of those authors, tell them that you are a writer, and ask if they are willing to read a snippet of your work and possibly recommend you to their agent. Rarely will an author pass something on to their agent that they are not feeling themselves, so do not simply ask for their agent's contact information; you can get that another way. Do take the time to craft the perfect query letter, synopsis, and consecutive sample chapters to send to an agent. Keep it professional and do not send anything in fancy packaging or send a gift basket that you believe to be creative enough to put you ahead of the pack. Agents care about your talent and then, if you pass that litmus test, they care about your attitude and demeanor.

In the next chapter on publishers, I talk about realistic contractual points in traditional publishing. If your agent appears to want to make a lot of demands that are not typical, you need to be careful. Unless you are a seasoned author who has sold tons of books, or you have a unique book that publishers are willing to go to war over (which rarely happens), or you are a major celebrity (and I do mean major celebrity), it is not going to happen. A publisher has no reason to cave in, shave off their bottom-line profits, or bend over backward for any writer when there are tens of thousands of talented and gifted people vying for a publishing deal on any given day.

All of that is to say, make sure that any agent you deal with is the coach, cheerleader, and campaigner that you need.

CHAPTER 11

Publishers

The competition to get into a publishing house is thick. You have to have accomplished something amazing in order to have publishing houses scrambling and worrying about trying to add you to their list. You either have to be someone famous—extremely famous—and in the media a lot, especially as of late; or be someone who has overcome some type of life-threatening situation, such as surviving in the Himalayas for a month without food or water; or be someone who has some kind of scandalous background with a celebrity who the public is dying to hear about; or be someone who has already sold tens to hundreds of thousands of books on your own, and the only way to go is up. That about sums it up. Outside of that, you are one of hundreds of thousands of people, maybe even millions, who want to become a published author.

So how do you get a publisher to notice you? We already discussed the importance and role of an agent. Sometimes the rejections come because of the following:

1. The publisher already has a full list for the next couple of years. In theory, most imprints do not have a set number of books they do yearly, but common sense dictates how many titles the staff of the imprint can bear without too much quality control being lost; each author needs attention. For me, that maximum number hovers right around sixty books per year, but I have published both more and less over the years. Other imprints do double or triple that number, and some do one-tenth of that number. It depends on the publisher's overall vision. All of that is to say that your book may have arrived at the wrong time.

2. Similar to scheduling issues, your book may be too closely related in topic to a book that the publisher already has on their upcoming slate. That happens with the Strebor imprint all the time. Plus, I refuse to put two books in the same genre out in the same month, so sometimes we get a book that is way too similar to another title and we reject it. Even with some of our current authors, if one turns in a

synopsis that is close to a book we have published before, or have slated for publishing, we will suggest that they write something else and possibly publish the originally submitted book two or three years down the road.

3. Your agent has tried to negotiate an advance that the publisher is not willing to pay. They do not feel like it is worth the risk. The publisher may have a standard rate for new authors and realize that they can get another book for that amount without taking the added financial risk. Or based on tracking sales of other titles in that particular genre, they do not believe the book can be profitable enough for them to publish it.

4. The book topic is not something that they are willing to publish, it is not their area of interest, or they simply have not had enough time to review it and will pass so you will not be held up from seeking another deal. This is a big one for me. I am amazed at the number of people who will submit something and expect an answer by the next week, or even the next month. It does not mean that we are not working diligently to read submissions; it means that you are not the only one and you have to wait your turn. I have even had some authors on my slate grow impatient, fire their agents, and

seek other deals. A couple found deals, but their careers eventually took a nosedive because of their impatience. More than once I planned to actually make an offer the very day that they sent a scathing email, "dismissing me" as their publisher. Them moving on only opened up an opportunity and space for someone else who was more appreciative of me—someone who had been patient.

Publishers are the ones taking 100 percent of the financial risk when it comes to your book. You are taking no financial risk. In fact, you are being paid without having sold a single book for them. There is this assumption that once you write a book, publishers should have to pay you thousands, tens of thousands, or hundreds of thousands because you took the initiative to pursue your passion and write a manuscript.

Most books never sell more than ten thousand copies.

For ten thousand copies of a trade paperback book, based on a retail cost of fifteen dollars and the industry standard royalty rate of 7.5 percent, you are looking at earning about $11,250—if you are lucky enough to sell that number. Not much money considering what it takes to support yourself and your family.

In your mind, you are probably saying to yourself that ten thousand books at a retail cost of fifteen dollars totals $150,000, and you are being screwed. You are presuming that the publisher is going to walk away with the other

$138,750. What you might not be factoring in is what it costs for the publisher to produce and market your work—including the expense of paying salaries, office overhead, and many other line items that are a part of the cost of doing business.

The publisher has to incur the expense of editing the book. Depending on its length, that could be anywhere from $1,000 to $4,000. Freelance editors charge differently—some by the page, others by the hour. Let's meet that number in the middle and say $2,500 for editing. That makes it $5,500 down for the publisher, $3,000 up for the writer. First pass pages are sent back to the writer for adjustments and include suggestions, omissions, additions, etc. Yes, that means you are actually expected to go over your work, diva! Then the book goes back to a copyeditor and the publisher incurs an additional expense of at least $1,000, putting them $6,500 in the hole.

The next step is cover design, which can range anywhere from $1,000 to $3,000. Then there is the interior layout design, around $2,000 more. Paying someone to write the catalog and back cover copy: an additional expense. Printing the book information in a catalog: an additional expense. Feeding the information out to various online bookselling sites: an additional expense. Presales conference, sales conference, and sending sales reps out into the field: additional expenses. Let's just say that at least 10 percent of that $150,000 is eaten up by these various elements.

Now it is time for the publisher to incur the expense of

printing your book at one printer, printing your cover at another printer, paying for both the interior and exterior parts to be sent to a bindery to be perfect bound, and then paying for the books to be shipped to the warehouse. For 10,000 books, we are talking roughly $20,000 to $25,000 for all of that, depending on the page count. The publisher is $35,000 to $40,000 in the hole. The pressure is rising, right?

It is now time to distribute your book. Bookstores get anywhere between 40–45 percent off the cover price when they place orders, depending on the volume ordered and whether or not they have a returnable or nonreturnable situation with the publisher. So that means $60,000 to $67,500 goes down the drain right there, whether it is a bookstore or online retailer such as Amazon.com. Now we have arrived at two-thirds of the retail costs or more being depleted before a single book leaves the shelves. Are you beginning to get a better picture as to why it is ridiculous to make the statement that publishers are walking away with the majority of money from your book? Like I said, the publisher is absorbing 100 percent of the financial risk.

This is merely a partial breakdown of what it takes to publish a book. Some authors will turn around and get upset when publishers are not willing to invest tens of thousands of additional money in publicity, marketing, and sending them on book tours—not to mention paying the average three hundred dollars per signing co-op fee that most bookstores charge for signings. If you go to a book signing and sell ten or fewer books, you are not even making back half of the cost to hold the signing. Sure, it feels good to go out and meet your fans, connect to your readers, etc.—if they actually show up, or even know about the signing. But at the end of the day, publishing is a business.

When it comes to contracts, they can vary but certain elements are generally the same:

1. The publisher acquires certain rights to the book in all formats, including ebook. The royalty rates vary for hardcover, trade paperback, mass market, and ebook.

2. The publisher negotiates to license certain rights to your work, like audio, large print, and book club rights, and then shares the proceeds with you at standard splits.

3. Most publishers have no interest in owning the film rights, since publishers are in the business of books, not movies. But companies are experimenting with more involvement in film. So we may see more of that in the future.

4. There will be a due date for the manuscript to be delivered and most contracts give the publisher up to eighteen months after the manuscript has been delivered and accepted to actually publish the book.

5. There will be a clause that states if the book is not turned in on time, or is not determined to be publishable, that the contract can be terminated and the advance will have to be returned. That's why the language is "delivery and acceptance."

6. You will have to state that you are the owner and creator of the work.

7. The publisher will maintain the right to hold back part of the royalties per statement period (usually twice a year) in order to account for returns. Returns refers to the industry practice allowing booksellers to return unsold inventory. An average of 40 percent of the books ordered by retailer are returned. The publisher will also be able to remainder—or sell at a reduced rate—the book to wholesalers in order to try to recoup some of the monies lost.

8. The publisher will want an option on your next work, but will probably be specific that it is the next work of a book of similar nature (this applies to fiction and nonfiction).

9. There will be an arbitration clause.

10. There will be a copyright clause.

Outside of those ten things, the terms of the contract will vary. The payout of the advance will vary as well. For hardcover books, you are normally paid a portion on signing, a portion on delivery and acceptance, a portion on publication of the hardcover edition, and a portion on publication of the trade paperback edition. You and/or your agent can negotiate how that is paid out.

Now I will tell you this, and it is not an exaggeration: if you do not earn the publisher a profit, you will probably not be published again. There are some publishers who will continue to take chances if they truly believe in the author, but eventually someone else will step in and shut that down if the company has lost too much money on you. I am not saying you should not desire an advance. I am saying the following:

1. An advance is just that: prepayment of money that you are expected to earn from your book. You will not see a dime beyond that amount until the threshold number of books sold earn back the advance and then some. There are a lot of writers who complain and blame the publisher when their royalty checks are small or nonexistent. That's because they have not earned back their advance.

2. If you do not earn out the advance, the chances of your publisher (or another publisher) taking a risk on you again will be slim. Better to receive a lower

advance that makes your chances of earning out better.

3. You need to realize that you are lucky to even have a publishing deal.

Publishing is a very small, close-knit world. Developing a reputation of being difficult to deal with, whether it is with your publisher, bookstores, book clubs, or other authors, will backfire on you. Saying something behind a publisher's back is pointless; you might as well say it to their face because they will know you said it in less than a week tops.

Trying to go over your editor or publicist's head to make them look bad is also not a good look. It only makes you look bad. I have had writers try to go over my head. Once they receive a reply reminding them of that, or receive no reply at all, it becomes clear. If I am the one who gave you a book deal, I am the one who is in your corner, and while the other people in the company may have heard of you, no one necessarily needs you around.

It has certainly been an interesting journey, and there have been times when I considered walking away. But then I realized that I love being a publisher, even though I could have spent the time writing two or three dozen additional books myself with the energy I have expended on others. That brings me to marketing and publicity.

One of the biggest complaints that authors have is that they feel marketing and publicity are not doing the best they can for them. Let me clarify something for you: most publicists work their asses off, during and after business hours. They cannot make people put you on television, they cannot make someone review your book, they cannot make a radio personality interview you, and they cannot work magic.

They send out galleys (advanced reading copies) to their connections, they follow up with phone calls and emails, they send a finished copy of the book upon release to the same people again, and they pitch you and/or your book everywhere that they possibly can. If you think the process is tough for you, imagine how they feel, especially when authors are constantly talking down to them and trying to lodge complaints against them.

I am the complete opposite. I will ask if something is possible and if my publicist comes back and says that it is not, I accept it and move on.

The efforts that the marketing department makes on the behalf of authors is rarely seen by the authors, but they work extremely hard as well. Everyone has budgets, though. Everyone hopes that new writers will take off. But a lot depends on the performance of the book in the weeks right after publication. If that happens, more money and energy is allocated toward marketing and publicity. The key is to help your publisher help you by taking as much initiative as you can in promoting and marketing your book.

The Bottom Line

Publishers do three main things:

1. Acquire new titles and negotiate contracts

2. Professionally edit, organize a timeline, manage and produce the book projects

3. Distribute and market the products

None of it is easy.

If you do not have an agent, have an attorney look over the contract. I have seen some ridiculous contracts that people signed with independent presses and then later regretted it. If you sense something is wrong, it probably is, and you should not sign until you feel totally comfortable.

People who are up to something generally pressure you to sign a contract within hours or days of receiving it—not a good sign. There are reasons and circumstances where signing a contract within a reasonable and certain amount of time is important, including the need to publish relatively quickly. We cannot, for example, begin the editorial and production work in earnest without a fully executed and signed contract.

It is a blessing to receive a publishing deal from a good

publisher. It means that you are being given an opportunity that others would cut off a limb to get. Someone believes in you enough to spend a lot of money on your work and see what happens, with no guarantees of making that money back in return. Do not take that for granted.

CHAPTER 12

Increasing Your Readership Base

At the end of the previous chapter on publishers, I mentioned the importance of writers being at least half responsible for their marketing and publicity efforts. Now I will go more in-depth about that in this chapter.

For the first five years of my writing career, not many people knew that I was Zane—not even my parents. I didn't do public appearances, do book signings, or post my photo. To this day, my actual photo is only on a couple of my books, even though there are thousands of pictures of me online. I have been in dozens of magazines and newspapers, six documentaries, and my portrait is touring to national museums. I do not have any interest in actually being famous, but there is nothing wrong with that for those who desire it. I write and publish because I am passionate about the art.

Now, a lot of people assume that the second their book is released, people will automatically line up to purchase it and fight over the last copy. Some authors never give marketing a second thought until they get a reality check. They think their work begins and ends with making editorial changes to their manuscripts, and then they wait for the "big day" to arrive. Then there are some who put forth some minor efforts online via Twitter and Facebook and then quickly give up altogether if they do not land on the bestseller lists. I have even seen celebrities do books and then give up quickly if it means having to put forth additional effort outside of what they already do. They assume that because they are famous their books will sell. The majority of celebrity books flop, and I have begun to shy away from them as a publisher for two reasons: 1) Most celebrities have too high expectations and make way too many assumptions about the roles they need to play in order to make their books a success, and 2) It is not economically beneficial to pay them bigger advances for books when they are not selling any more books than authors who have busted their behinds to write and deserve the chance.

Most people are not celebrities; they are ordinary, everyday people who want to share their talent with the world. But how is that done? Through a sacrifice of time, effort, and dedication. The same three things that it takes to be successful in other industries.

I see some authors grow hysterical if a reader says something they do not agree with, or if they get a bad review. They go online and paste it on a social network and wait for their readers to defend their wonderful books. Sure, some people will hop on the post and cosign on their anger, but most people are looking at the post and shaking their heads. It is a sign of immaturity to get upset about negativity toward your work. Take pride in your work regardless. If you believe you put your best effort into the book and it is a compelling story, carry yourself that way. Let it slide right off of you. Do not engage in arguments with readers and book reviewers, in private or in front of anyone else. Either do not respond, or thank them for giving your work a chance, like I do.

Going hand in hand with not engaging in foolishness with readers and reviewers is refraining from getting caught up in drama with other authors. The drama will rear its ugly head, even if you put out your first book last week. Sometimes it will start before your first book even comes out. A lot of authors treat this business like a reality show or an elimination competition. They believe that they have to try to get other authors out of their way so they can win the grand prize. They will attempt to sabotage other authors by defaming them, posting fake reviews under various names online, and sometimes coming straight out and inciting an argument about nothing.

Authors have complained to bookstores and distributors about me, demanding that they sell more of their books than mine. What they are not getting is that no one can make readers purchase a book. They have gone into bookstores and asked why my book was in the front window when they were the ones there to do a signing. Mind you, their books were on display someplace because they were there to do a signing. I have walked into industry events and it seemed like the air was sucked out of the room all of a sudden, to the point where I simply have to say my hellos and leave.

All of that is to say that instead of treating other writers like your fellow contestants on *Big Brother* or *Survivor*, treat them like your teammates and work together to win the championship ring. Even if professional athletes cannot stand one another and have all kinds of drama off the field, when they get on the field, all of that is thrown out of the window. They have a common goal—winning—and they realize that they have to work together to achieve it. You are doing yourself a great disservice by treating other authors like your competition.

You need to work together to build your readership. You need to share ideas, exactly like I am doing in this entire book. I am not taking anything away from my own writing career by sharing what I know. With that being said, here are the key ways to grow your readership base.

Book Fairs and Conferences

Book fairs and conferences are amazing places to connect with readers and others in the industry. Meeting you in person and seeing your pleasant personality and humility in action has a big impact on their buying decisions. That goes for both readers and acquisitions editors/publishers who may be in attendance.

They are also great places to gain more knowledge about writing and the overall industry, if you are serious about longevity and establishing a career. I have met at least two dozen authors at such places that I either ended up publishing or ended up referring to agents or other publishers.

A lot of authors automatically opt out of attending book fairs and conferences if they are not selected to be on a panel discussion or are not a featured author. After all, their book fits right into one of the topics, so how dare the organizers not include them? You need to get over that, fast, quick, and in a hurry.

I realize that it is easy to say that it is not worth attending, especially if you have to travel and are not guaranteed to sell a lot of books. In some cases, you may not sell a single book, even if you pay for a vending table or booth. There it is: the cold hard truth. However, it is worth more than the book sales if you establish contact with a single person who can have a positive effect on your career.

Even if you hand out bookmarks, it is better than

nothing. Most of the bookmarks will be disregarded or discarded, but not all of them. Someone might get your bookmark and not purchase your book until two years later when they run across the bookmark or see your book online or in a store, or even hear someone else discussing it. The key is that your name and the title of your book have been implanted in their heads.

Also, make sure that you meet the organizers of the event and express your interest in being featured at the next one. Volunteer to help if they need any assistance. If you ingratiate yourself to them, chances are something will come from that. What you should not do is approach them with an attitude and show animosity over not being one of the chosen few, or imply that you are better qualified to speak than the people showcased. All you are doing there is making sure that you will never be selected. They do not know you; therefore you should not take things like that personally.

Connect with organizers and ask them for advice, or ask if they want to team up and do some things together. Compliment them on what they said, if you actually took the time out to listen and you believe it was positive information. Tell them that their books sound interesting, and yes, purchase their books if you are so inclined. I am known for signing at an event and going down the line and getting every other author to autograph a book for me so I can purchase them. It is a way of showing my support for their efforts, even if people are walking by them like they do not even exist.

Do the best that you can with the opportunity that you have been presented. Success often occurs when opportunity meets preparation. If you are not doing anything else that day, and you can figure out a way to be there, definitely attend and get your face, name, and pleasant and humble personality out there. I keep pointing out the personality for a reason.

Libraries

Connecting with libraries can be major. Go to several in person and inquire about doing signings or events on their sites. Ask if you can even start a book club there, if they do not have one. Visit them on a regular basis and gain their support. Send librarians greeting cards and let them know you appreciate them, even if you are not convinced they have purchased one copy of your book. It might inspire them to do so. A lot of librarians are overwhelmed and trying to keep up with the pace, but if you offer to help organize something they will likely jump on the opportunity since it will make them appear more active in the community. Before long, they will be calling on you to suggest things you can do together. All of that will help to increase your exposure and show that you are open to supporting other authors as well. Definitely a good look. After all, every author should be an avid reader first. The desire to even write a book should stem from an appreciation of other books.

Book Clubs

If you can get in with the right book clubs, you will have it made for your current and future books. Some of them will even pay for you to come to their hometown for each book, put you up in a hotel, feed you, and organize local events that include other local book clubs. A lot of authors will not even "consider" a book club if it only has a few members. They want to only appear in front of larger groups. Huge mistake! Stop being so pressed about selling dozens of books with each outing.

The one thing that you are guaranteed to find with book clubs are people who love to read and people who love to discuss what they read. That means if they like your book, not only will they discuss it among themselves, they will tell anyone who will listen about your writing: their friends, relatives, and coworkers. Going to a book club meeting with five members could lead to five hundred book sales before it is all over. They provide you with free word-of-mouth advertising, and if you are a likable person, they will practically feel obligated to help you achieve your goals.

What you should not do is approach a bunch of book clubs and *insist* that they choose your book for their monthly meeting. You have to entice them to want to select your book. The way that happens is by connecting with them as human beings, and not potential sales. The book club situation is not going to work for people who only write to make money, though. If that is you, forget about it. You need to be as passionate about books as they are and be willing to discuss other writers if the occasion arises.

Also, if you cannot take criticism well, do not do book club meetings *at all*. You are asking for a series of disasters. Not every member of the book club is going to like your book. Even if they do like it, there will probably be at least one member there that day who got up on the wrong side of the bed, or a member who has always wanted to be a published author and feels like you are not as good of a writer as her (mind you that she has taken no actual steps to become a writer), or one member who has a nasty attitude all the time (the other members tolerate her because she is related or they are trying to keep her mind off other things).

When someone says something negative about your work to your face, when they question your storyline choices or say they could not connect to any of your characters, you cannot go on the defensive. They are entitled to their opinions, and their opinions are what they are. You have no other choice but to accept them. You should address their questions and concerns, though. After all, you placed yourself into the position and agreed to do a book club "discussion." But you should respond in a confident, uplifting way. If you do it correctly, you may actually win them over. Even the most sarcastic of people are impressed when someone takes their attacks in stride and handles the situation calmly and professionally.

Book clubs are rather easy to find. They actually want to

be found. They are proud of the fact that they are organized and supportive readers and want the world to know it. Many of them have Facebook pages and Twitter accounts, as well as individual websites. Several of them offer to do reviews of your books and post them on various sites. They have submission guidelines and tell you where to send them. I highly suggest you do that. It means giving away a free book, but if you get a review from a well-known club or reviewer, it cannot hurt.

However—there is always a however—if the review is not to your liking, you have to control yourself. Do not email or call them asking that it be removed. Do not put a link to the negative review on your Facebook page and try to make the reviewer look bad. If they say something about your book being poorly edited, it probably is, and you are upset because you did not want anyone to point that out. If they say that the book seemed rushed and the storyline was not cohesive, you need to ask yourself if any of that may be true. Even if none of it is true, it is the way that they viewed the book, you solicited the review, and they spent valuable hours of their time reading it. You need to appreciate that.

A lot of book clubs are using Skype to conduct discussions now. You can do it from the comfort of your own home or office. If you can do that and not have to travel, find a sitter, etc., then there is no reason for you not to do it, even if the club has a handful of members. The fact that they even read your book and want to talk about it with you speaks volumes. You should appreciate that.

Mailing Lists

Even if you have Facebook, Twitter, Google+, etc., I still highly recommend maintaining mailing lists, both snail mail and email lists. If you have sold your books directly to people in the past, keep their mailing addresses and send them postcards on the regular and holiday cards. In fact, find out their birthdays and send them birthday cards. Also have a mailing list of local salons, independent stores, and barber shops where you can send postcards for your new titles, or postcards with a collage of your titles on them, even if it is just to say, "I hope you are having a good summer." Little things like this make a huge difference.

As for email lists, they are a direct way to connect with your readers without having to worry about them missing your tweet or Facebook post. Not everyone is glued to those two sites all day, every day. It is currently three-thirty p.m. in Maryland as I type this, and I have yet to go online at all today. That means anything posted on those two sites so far today I will likely not even see. From personal experience, I can tell you that no matter how many times you post something, not everyone will see it. I will post ten times that I am doing a signing at a Philadelphia library, and the next day people are posting on my page asking when I am coming to Philadelphia. The same goes for Atlanta, NYC, Chicago—everywhere. With a mailing list, you can send them the information directly and they will open it when they check their inbox.

Your email list should not be used to bombard your subscribers with promotional material. I suggest sending out one about your books no more than once a month. A weekly newsletter is a good idea but it should be about current events, recommending books by other authors, writing tips, and providing exclusive rewards and promotions. I have sent an email out merely to tell all of my subscribers that I love and appreciate them and want them to know it. Something weighed heavily on my heart, telling me to send it. The next day a woman emailed me and told me that she was about to kill herself over a man the day before until she read my email. We ended up connecting many times to discuss what she was going through.

My point is that your readers need to feel like you care. More importantly, you should care. Mine mean the world to me, not only because they purchase my books but because I enjoy vibing with them. After all, if you have no readers, you are only writing for yourself.

Mailing lists are also a great place to send out excerpts of your books. The reason my books did so well right out of the gate is because I gave away excerpts of my writing for three years before I ever published a book. In fact, I never really planned to publish a book until a rumor got started. People emailed me saying that they had been looking for my book all over and had inquired at bookstore chains in an effort to locate it. I am not sure where the belief came from that I had a published book, but it definitely did not come from me.

Organizations and Local Businesses

Depending on what your book is about, you may be able to connect with various local and national organizations to speak to their members. Start with ones that you are a member of, like sororities, fraternities, and professional organizations. Many of them have annual conventions. So do churches, women's groups, men's groups, and just about any kind of group you can think of. Many, if not most, will be receptive to having you attend if you offer and make yourself seem knowledgeable.

It may come down to your acquiring a vending space. You have to weigh the expense with the potential profit margin and see if it makes sense. No matter what, you are going to have to invest in your writing career. I understand that a lot of people do not have extra funds. In that case, try to connect with them on the Internet; ask if you can be a guest or even permanent blogger on their website.

If you can get in good with a major organization, you could sell hundreds or thousands of books if the members embrace you. Volunteer to help with their projects. That means networking and meeting new people. The more people you meet, the better.

Local businesses like restaurants, salons, and retail stores are often open to allowing you to do book signings. I will even tell you a secret, but keep it quiet. Most major retailers have policies in place for their individual stores to do regular, community-related events on a monthly basis. Most of the locations don't do it because the managers are too overwhelmed to go out and find people to invite, or to add event planning to their workload. But if you go in there and ask, they will let you do it since you were bold enough to come in and ask.

Other Authors

Fellow authors can really do a lot to help one another catapult their careers. As a publisher of hundreds of books, over the years we have had a few powerful author teams in-house who traveled together, marketed together, and extended overall support to one another. It works well.

I am not suggesting that you try to hook up with every author under the sun. There should be a level of mutual respect, chemistry, and admiration for it to make sense. But if you find such people to team up with, you should cross-promote each other's work, introduce them to your industry connections, such as radio personalities, bloggers, and reporters, and come up with sweepstakes and giveaways that you can do together.

If you find other authors in your local area, you can host book club events, seminars, and book signings together. Two people doing a book signing draw more attention than one. It does not mean that every person will purchase both of your books, but you will probably get some good sales out of it. Once a person finishes talking to you, introduce them to the other person by stating their name and handing the reader a copy of their book.

Engage in conversations together on social media networks and tag each other in posts so that their readers can learn more about you and vice versa. Speaking of social media, I saved the best for last.

Various Websites

Most media-based websites, book-based websites, and book-blogging sites are constantly looking for content. After all, that is what drives their traffic. If they do not update their material—sometimes several times a day—people will stop coming. Therefore, it cannot hurt to offer to be a guest blogger on those sites in exchange for their putting a link up for your book.

Also, you should approach sites that deal with the particular genre or topic of your book. You have to think outside of the box, and the ultimate power is in numbers. The more people who you are exposed to, the more possible readers you will gain. Offer to do a weekly column, advice column, or offer to provide them with excerpts of your work. Obviously, if people enjoy the excerpt, they will be anxious to read the book. You should take this seriously and develop a spreadsheet of people to reach out to, keep track of, and follow up with. Keep detailed notes on any interaction you have with them. In fact, you should set up a separate email folder for "leads." This truly is a business and it must be regarded as such. You are a salesperson. Never forget that.

Social Media

While it may be plausible to sell a lot of books in today's climate without being active on social media, it is very rare, and normally only happens if the author is connected enough to be featured on a national morning show, afternoon talk show, or late-night show. Those are a select few, and it is more based on who they know than what they have written or done. It is clearly not done on the basis of accomplishments.

So those of us who do not fit into their selection process must fend for ourselves. I actually love social media. Then again, I started out my career online and have a gift for gab. But here is the thing: I talk about my books less than anything else. Yet I have hundreds of thousands of followers. I connect to them in ways that have nothing to do with writing.

You have to do more than post about your books. After the fifth or sixth time, people will either ignore you altogether or unfollow or unlike you. They know your book is out and heard you the first time.

So what are you supposed to be doing on the Internet? Market yourself and not your book. Here is the thing: if you talk about things that people want to hear, they will be curious about what you have to say in your books. But it needs to be genuine. I did not start out with the idea of marketing myself on the Internet. On the contrary, I did not even want anyone to know who I was. What happened is a true testament to the power of the Internet.

Back before there was a Facebook, a Twitter, or even a MySpace, I started writing these short stories and posting them on my free AOL web space, then on the ACLU Black Erotica Board, then on Eroticanoir.com, which I started sometime in early 1999. I was having fun, talking to people, being myself, and at the same time having the freedom of speech to say things that I would never say to people whom I knew in real life.

Early on in the process, I only had a few stories posted. No website. I was home late one night in a rural and remote part of North Carolina when one of my friends showed up on my doorstep, banging on the door. She was quite excited and I thought something was wrong. Come to find out that she had just left her second-shift job at Freightliner Trucks, on the assembly line, and she was excited because she wanted me to read something. She said that some guys at her job had printed it out and everyone was passing it around and that I had to read it.

When I looked down at the crumpled pieces of paper, I realized that it was one of my short stories—"The Airport," to be exact. I had to try to pretend that I had never heard of this "Zane" person, but I did not think that I could pull it off sitting there and reading it in front of her like I did not know it by heart, word for word. I told her that I would read it in the morning since I was exhausted, and she left. That night was the first time that I realized that Zane—my alter ego—was taking on a life of her own. And she was doing it as I sat in a small, three-bedroom brick house in the country.

I decided to do a test and offered up ten of my short stories for ten dollars plus three dollars shipping and handling. I put the offer on my website with a PO Box and sat back and waited. It did not take long. I was flooded with orders, to the point that I found myself in the office supply store making more copies on a daily basis. It became clear that if people were willing to send me thirteen dollars for what amounted to fifty photocopied pages, I could actually sell a book. Yet, I hesitated.

I eventually moved back to the DC area but no one knew who I was. I got a job in corporate America and continued to write in my spare time. But Zane continued to gain more and more readers. I enjoyed doing the monthly newsletters, vibing with different authors and even book clubs, although I did not have a book out. More and more people were joining my email list, people were talking about my writing all over the Internet, and one of the sex manuals I wrote ended up in my inbox no less than fifty times.

Today, it is even easier to go viral as a writer. Back when I started, authors had to drive traffic to their individual websites, or convince people to subscribe to their email lists. Some writers have grown lazy because of social networking and/or they do not understand that people do not like to be spammed. If you engage in actual conversations, comment on the pages of others, post witty sayings or quotes, and pass on interesting articles, your likes and followers will grow. The key is to post things that people will share. That may drive others to visit your page and join.

Earlier this week, I posted a photo of my soon-to-be-ninety-five-year-old aunt. By that night, she had more than six thousand comments, 95,000 likes, and more than 1.4 million people had viewed the picture. I received an email from a production company in California asking if she might be interested in being one of the subjects for a documentary they are doing on elders. In less than a day, my aunt became a famous woman. That is the power of the Internet.

Let me be clear about one thing: I am not suggesting that you stay on the Internet day in and day out. You would never get anything done. Some people assume that I am on there all the time but I use scheduling software for my posts. When I am at a book signing, people laugh because they just got a notification of a new post from me, yet I am clearly nowhere near a computer or phone to post. I would suggest spending no more than an hour a day on the Internet. Outside of that, you are losing valuable productivity time and it is easy to get addicted. If you are writing three or four thousand words a day on various social networks and writing five hundred words a day on your next book, that is a problem. You have to maintain a healthy balance. Regard it like you do a teenager who arrives for their first year of college. They have to learn to balance a social life and their schoolwork. Otherwise, they will end up as one of those people who dropped out or were expelled after their freshman year. Just like college, some people can party all the time, hang out on the yard, and seem to be at every event on campus, and still maintain good grades. That is because they stay up all night studying or have a photographic memory. Not everyone can do that.

I also want to stress that you should use social networking responsibly. Do not put too much of your personal business on the Internet, no matter what career you have. Do not show animosity toward anyone else on social networking and get caught up in drama. Not only are potential readers looking, potential publishers, filmmakers, producers, business partners, and all others are also looking. Social networking can be your greatest friend or your greatest enemy.

The Bottom Line

Readers are not going to fall into your lap. A few might initially, but most will find you in another way. You cannot solely rely on other people to spread the word about your talent. You have to be your greatest cheerleader, campaigner, and coordinator. If you do not feel comfortable doing many of the things that I listed in this chapter, enlist the help of a friend or relative who loves to plan events, loves to travel, and loves to connect with the masses online. Find someone who practically lives on social networks and ask them to manage your pages for you. They will probably be flattered and feel important. If you have teenagers, put them to work as well. Do whatever it takes, but never give up. This is a marathon, not a sprint, but it is well worth it in the end.

CHAPTER 13

Distribution Outlets

Even if one creates the most amazing intellectual property ever, without ways to distribute it, most of the world will never even know it exists. We have gone over how to increase your readership base, how to use social networking to your advantage, and the importance of attending conferences and connecting with book clubs. Now we need to discuss ways that all of your prospective readers can obtain your work.

Although the tides have begun to shift from print to digital books, hard copy books still sell extremely well. Not everyone is content to read electronic books. My parents, for example, have never read an ebook and they are the most avid readers that I have ever known. Both retired educators,

I grew up in a house with a basement full of anywhere from eight thousand to ten thousand books on any given day. Like myself, my father has written dozens of books and he reads all of the time, even well into his eighties. But he reads hard copy books only.

Therefore, the bookstores are still important for new authors to be discovered. A lot of readers make impulse buys by scanning shelves and selecting something that sparks their interest. Most of my favorite writers were discovered in that very way. I was in a bookstore and my eyes were drawn to a book so I picked it up, liked the title, thought the cover was intriguing, read the back, and I was on my way. It is easier for an author to attract attention when they have numerous titles on the shelf—maybe even the entire shelf. It makes someone wonder what their writing style must be like.

It is getting harder and harder to get a book into bookstores. Keeping it real, the task has always been more difficult for African-American authors. Even those of us who are *New York Times* bestsellers do not make it on the end caps of major stores, even when those stores are in predominately African-American communities. Therefore, other authors have an unfair advantage over those of us who have worked just as hard, churned out just as much material, and deserve the same opportunity to be discovered by potentially new readers. In many library systems, I am the most circulated author. I have two cable series and a feature film. Yet I am shunned by major chains; if they have my books at all, it is usually one or two titles and they are on a side shelf. Most airport stores do not carry my own, or any other African-American authors' books for that matter, but they will carry a book by a completely new author who writes in the same genre that I do. It is easy to make the bestseller list when your book is showcased in a hundred times more stores.

I am not going to paint a pretty picture about it being easy to get a book into bookstores and major department stores. That goes double for grocery stores. I have seen my own titles in two grocery stores over the years. There is blatant racism when it comes to African-American books being offered to the consumers in stores. Quite frankly, being that we spend hundreds of millions of dollars as a community yearly on books, that is one reason why some stores are currently struggling or no longer in business. Maybe if they offered more of what their direct consumers wanted to purchase, their sales would improve. It is totally different when it comes to music and film. CDs by popular African-American artists and movies featuring African-American movie stars are quickly put on end caps, even by the registers, and not only in predominantly African-American communities, but in all communities. It implies that buyers and managers at these chains—possibly even top-level executives—believe that African-Americans listen to music and watch movies but do not read. I am not saying this because I harbor some type of bitterness toward stores. I accepted the obvious after my first *New York Times* bestseller. However, as a publisher of dozens of titles per year, it disturbs me greatly.

Now, we do have books in some stores, but the imbalance is obvious. Some of you will be able to have your books placed everywhere and others—including myself—will have to deal with the consequences of our skin color and the social climate of the country.

If you are published by a traditional house, they will take care of selling your book to stores. But it never hurts to visit your local stores and let your presence be known. A lot of chains have cut back on book signings and a lot of publishers have stopped sending authors on tour because it's not economically sound. The stores have to order dozens of books, sometimes hundreds, and if the author has more than one title, they have to advertise, have key personnel allocated for the event, and then hope people actually show up. Publishers have to pay hundreds of dollars to the store for the signing, transport the author to town, pay for a media escort or limousine, and a hotel room, pay for promotional posters, and then hope people actually show up. The tricky part now is that even if there is a big crowd, a lot of people now simply come out to meet the author and say that they are going to buy the ebook. It is fine if they want to read the book electronically, but that deducts from the logic of the author being there in the first place. While the author may enjoy connecting with readers—I love it—the bottom line is that the event is in the red and everyone is upset.

After my last book tour in fall 2012, I realized that I never wanted to do another official tour. Even though I got to see a couple dozen cities, even the Cayman Islands, there were too many hits and misses. I had a great turnout at about half of the events. At some of the libraries there were hundreds of people, and the store in the Caymans said it was the largest signing they had ever had. They moved my speech to a local movie theater. It was an amazing event, and hundreds of books were sold. But that was because that particular bookstore chain embraced me as an author—despite my skin color—and went all out to make it a success. They realized that *all* of their consumers read my books, and the turnout was multicultural. My overall readership is multicultural, but a lot of stores fail to realize that and miss out on a lot of money. Again, one of the reasons that they are struggling is by overlooking the obvious. We live in an age where President Barack Obama won 43 percent of the white vote in 2008 and 39 percent of the white vote in 2012, but buyers at bookstores are still not convinced that white readers will and do read African-American authors. I do not believe that it will ever change.

When it comes to ebooks, by no means do I believe that they will completely take over. It will probably be similar to music. A lot of people these days listen to their music on their phones, tablets, or other devices, but some still listen to actual CDs. I listen to six CDs in rotation in my car. Ebooks are definitely a simple way for readers to get a book and start reading it immediately. It is also a great distribution method for those authors whose books cannot be found in bookstores anyway. If a reader goes to a store looking for a book and cannot find it, that really leaves them with three options: 1) make a special request for the book to be ordered and make an additional trip to come back and buy it; 2) order the book online and incur delivery/shipping expenses, and then wait for it to arrive; 3) download it and start reading it within the next sixty seconds. There is no question why it is appealing. People like instant gratification. They can get a book in seconds, a new song in seconds, a new movie in seconds, or hop on Netflix or Hulu and watch the latest releases in seconds.

If you want to succeed in this business long-term, you have to think outside of the box. There is no way around that. Therefore, you need to develop a business plan for your writing career; you have to start to think of yourself as a corporation and have a five-to-ten-year plan. It might sound complicated—even silly to some of you—but it is true. I did it and I became a brand. Now I am right smack in the middle of the second ten-year plan. The point is that I made it to the second plan by completing the first.

You have to set goals in your career and refuse to get frustrated if things fall off track. I will be the first to admit that things do not always happen when we want them to happen; they happen when they are supposed to happen. But I also believe in proactively pursuing your goals so you cannot sit back, relax, and assume your job is done once your book is released by a publisher. If you have self-published, you definitely cannot sit back and relax. While ebooks make it easy for people to get a book, they have to desire the book. You have to find ways to get your material out in front of the masses in various places. Not everyone is online, some people never go online, and not everyone frequents bookstores or the book sections in department stores. So where do your potential readers congregate? That is what you have to figure out.

Let's pretend that you have written a book on health and wellness—a huge area of interest and a multibillion-dollar industry. You should approach doctors' offices and see if they will allow you to leave some bookmarks on their counter, hang up a poster, or even leave a complimentary reading copy on their coffee table. Of course, you need to give the doctor and/or nurse an autographed copy for them to enjoy. If they enjoy it, they will promote it. If they like your personality, they will promote you.

You should approach your local gym, ask them if you can leave some material, and then take it a step further. Ask the gym manager if you can offer to conduct a weekly seminar on health and wellness free-of-charge in one of their exercise studios. You would be surprised how many would jump on that opportunity to offer something additional to their members. What you get out of it is book sales and the chance to establish yourself as an authority on the subject. Eventually, you can start expanding your seminar out to other local areas; if it becomes popular enough, you can expand to other major cities and states. Before long, people will be reaching out to you because someone they know attended one, thought it was great, and want to host one near them.

Another good idea is to connect with local health food stores. Do not limit yourself to smaller, independent stores. Go for broke and approach the manager of the local Whole Foods, Trader Joe's, or any grocery store chain around. Ask them if they will carry a few of your books in the store and see what happens. Ask if you can come in on Saturday afternoon and do a book signing. Ask. Ask. Ask. If one manager says no, ask the next one. If that manager says no, ask the next one. Every no will get you closer to a yes.

With the explosion of health and wellness network marketing companies, you need to approach their headquarters about possibly adding your book to their product list. Now most of you are probably thinking, *There is no damn way they would carry my book when all of these other books are out there! Why would they do that?* I can answer that: because you were the one bold enough to approach them and ask. If you can get your book into that type of situation, you are automatically talking about thousands of book sales per month. Isn't it worth the time to ask?

The Bottom Line

No matter what the topic of your book is, you can find ways to sell it outside conventional bookselling channels. If your book is about hair care, ask salon owners if they will offer your book for sale. If your book is about animals, ask veterinarians and even the local zoo if they will carry your book. If your book is about self-defense, ask local martial arts studios if they will carry your book. While you are at it, always ask if you can do some kind of event or seminar at their establishments. Better yet, going back to the health and wellness book for a minute, spend a few dollars and host a launch party for your book and invite all of your local targets—doctors, gym managers, store managers, and network marketers. You would be surprised how many of them will actually show up out of curiosity. At the end of the evening, act like you are willing to do them the favor of allowing them to carry your book.

If you make it sound like a hot commodity, they will be anxious to sell it. Even if you are just starting out, you have to claim victory and act like your book is the hottest thing to hit the market in a decade. You have to carry yourself with confidence and authority, and convince them that whatever you said in the book matches the intellectually stimulating conversation you are having with them in person. See how all of these elements come together into the perfect storm?

CHAPTER 14

Today's Publishing Climate

One of the few things in life that remains consistent is evolution. The way that we regard our situations and surroundings at the age of ten is totally different from how we comprehend things at twenty, thirty, forty, fifty, and so on. Just as a human being changes, so does the publishing industry.

There are many challenges now that did not even present themselves two to five years ago. Publishers, agents, booksellers, and authors are going to have to find a way to look years into the future and get ahead of the curve, or fall behind it. Grassroots marketing is even more crucial than before and much easier than before because of the Internet. Twenty-five years ago the World Wide Web did not even exist. Now it is a lifeline for billions of people to connect globally. The limitations that prevented authors from gaining readers around the world are gone. No longer do their books have to be picked up by a foreign publisher and/or printed, distributed, and shipped overseas. They can be downloaded.

Bookstores are disappearing. The independents have been practically annihilated because they could not compete with the discounted pricing of the larger chains. Customers refused to pay the extra 20 percent to support small business owners. Now the larger chains are being annihilated by the tax-free websites that offer even deeper discounts than they could offer. It is a butterfly effect.

The department stores, grocery stores, and airport stores will only stock and promote select authors, and not even the top-selling tier of authors but the authors who they have determined will appeal to their consumers, even when those consumers are the same race as the authors they refuse to carry. Some book reviewers have come right out and said that they do not review "black books," even when they previously sounded excited about the books when first approached based on the titles and synopses. And they have no reason to change as long as African-Americans continue to take the money out of our own community and patronize them.

That is why street vendors are so important. They are more supportive and appreciative of African-American books than anyone, and they sell a ton of books—money that stores could make but do not care to make, unless it is from peddling African-American films and music. But do not get me wrong, African-Americans are not the only ones slighted in this business. In some stores, we at least have our own "section." Of course, that prevents many new readers from discovering us.

I attended a Latino book festival years ago and the authors on the panel with me were in a panic and asking me for suggestions on how to get more exposure. They were upset that they did not have their own section in stores, and a strange feeling overcame me. I realized that this was what it was like before publishers started acquiring African-American titles in bulk.

Female authors are not given as much exposure as male authors across the board, no matter what the race. We are still considered to be the weaker sex in this country, and there are issues that we face when it comes to getting exposure and attention as well. As I go about my daily life, I feel like I am more discriminated against because I am female than because I am African-American. We truly have a long way to go, and we need to pull each other along the path together.

There is still much segregation going on in the literary world. Authors of other races can write entire series based on African-American characters and receive prime placement in stores. But when an African-American writes a book about other races, or a general topic, we tend to be placed in the "section."

I am not sure what will happen to the publishing industry in the future, but I am sure it will continue to evolve. It saddens me that so many people do the majority of communicating online. There is nothing like that face-to-face, voice-to-voice contact. That is why it is imperative that you remain active in the real world, connecting to people, even if you reside in a remote town and it is on a smaller scale. Remember what I said about the difference between being a writer and an author? If you want to last in this business, you have to master both roles.

I may not know you but I love and appreciate you for taking the time out to read this book. It has been a labor of love, but at least now I will not feel bad when I get email after email asking for writing tips. Now I can direct them to their local library or bookstore, depending on where this book is carried and sold. Like I said, this will truly be a testament to what is going on in the industry.

Thank you for the support, and I wish you nothing but the best in whatever path you take in life. Remember that the only limitations in life are the ones we place on ourselves. Even when others do try to block us, fail to support us, and act like we do not exist, we have to move past that and find another way to make it. Good luck, God bless, and get to writing!

PART 3

WRITING EXERCISES

This section is to help spark your imagination, push you outside of your comfort zone, and encourage you to think outside of the box. I include writing exercises designed not to be used just once, but over and over whenever you feel up to a challenge or have the nasty disease we refer to as "writer's block."

EXERCISE #1—
CHARACTER DEVELOPMENT

Pick one or two characters from your book, either one you have completed (if you are trying to work on a new one) or one you are currently writing. Write a two thousand– to three thousand–word short story where you become a part of their world and interact with them. Pretend like all of you are having dinner together at a restaurant or that you have been invited over to one of their homes for dinner. If your book is adventurous, go on a quest with them. If your book is a murder mystery or detective story, inject yourself into a crime scene. If your book is family-oriented, pretend you are one of the relatives.

The purpose of this exercise is to help you get to know your characters better. When I am penning a novel, I begin to stride when I start to actually live and breathe the characters. You need to be able to identify with your characters if you expect your readers to identify with them. If you find yourself stuck on a particular section of your book, take a break and do this.

EXERCISE #2—
CHARACTER DEVELOPMENT

Pretend like you are interviewing one of the focal characters of your book: either the protagonist or the antagonist. Actually prepare a list of fifteen to twenty questions to ask and put on your reporter's hat. After the questions are prepared, transport yourself into the psyche of that character and answer the questions. Outside of obvious background questions, like age, place of birth, etc., here are some suggested questions (random and based on various genres).

1. When was the first time that you realized you gained pleasure from killing people? (For serial killer.)

2. Did you ever imagine that you would sleep with so many men during the same time period when

you were a teenager? (For sexually uninhibited woman.)

3. What would you do if you found out that your wife is also cheating on you? (For married man carrying on an affair.)

4. Do you ever think you will get up the nerve to actually approach him and ask him out on a date? (For shy female.)

5. If you could travel anywhere in the world, where would you go and why? (For anyone.)

Allow your imagination to run free. This is a way to deepen your characters in a fun way without feeling a lot of pressure.

EXERCISE #3—
CHARACTER DEVELOPMENT

This is a really fun one. Have your protagonist and antagonist write blogs about each other. Showcase the issues they have with the other person and allow them to be strong in their opinions.

Take it a step further and have them go into things that happened in the past—their backstory. Even if none of that ends up in the book, it will help you, the writer, to understand them better. If you enjoy this, you can do it for all of the focal characters in your book.

EXERCISE #4—CHARACTER DEVELOPMENT

This exercise should have nothing to do with any of your actual characters. Actually, I want you to develop a character profile about a complete stranger, someone you cross paths with on the street, or in a store. Writers tend to be extremely observant so it should be easy to select someone on a whim.

Watch them for a few moments and memorize things about them. The way that they dress, their mannerisms, their facial expressions. Then I want you to go home and pretend like you know them—well. Write a sketch about who they are: name, age, occupation, marital status, etc. Before you know it, you will have developed an interesting character that you may actually be able to use in a future book. It may even spark you to start a new book.

EXERCISE #5—
CHARACTER DEVELOPMENT

Pretend like your character has decided to join an online dating site—even if they are married and prepared to creep—

and make up their dating profile. If you need a template, join any of the free sites for a day and scan through some of the profiles to see what information is shared.

What kind of photo would your character choose to put up? A conservative one or a sensual one? How would he or she describe themselves? What member name would he or she choose and why? What traits would he or she be looking for in a mate? What are his or her hobbies? Does he or she like to travel? Does he or she work out? What would he or she describe as the perfect date?

EXERCISE #6—
STORYLINE DEVELOPMENT

This exercise involves creating a storyline from a single photograph or piece of art. It can be a famous photograph or painting or any random one you see in a magazine or online. What matters most is that you select a scene that sparks your interest enough to write about it.

Once you choose one, write at two thousand– to three thousand–word short story about it. There does not even have to be any actual people in the scene. There could be a landscape, animals, or even animated characters. Whenever you are bored, you can do this, even if you merely spot an interesting photo on someone's timeline on a social network.

EXERCISE #7—
STORYLINE DEVELOPMENT

Pick a social problem and pretend like you are going to play an integral part in solving it. Outline the actions that you would take to make that happen. Decide whom you would need to assist and you what important roles they would play. Decide on a timeline and a deadline for when you must resolve this issue. Pick an issue that you are passionate about, like world hunger, domestic violence, unemployment, homelessness, or lack of health care.

Actually do research on the subject, find out who the key players are in the movement, and which politicians are pro or con about political reform. Do not give up until you have figured out a viable way to make the world a better place.

EXERCISE #8—
STORYLINE DEVELOPMENT

What is your greatest fear in life? Write a short story where you are the main character and you have to face that fear head on. What will be your first reaction? How would you handle it? Do you think you could even handle it? What would you draw on for strength? This is a good exercise for a couple of reasons: 1) it sparks the imagination; 2) you might actually overcome that fear, even if you do not actually have to face it in real life.

EXERCISE #9—
STORYLINE DEVELOPMENT

Write a story about your earliest childhood memory, but write it from the perspective of the age that you were at the time. The reason that I bring this up is because our earliest childhood memories must be significant for some reason, or we would not remember them. It is also a great idea because you can pass it on to your children or other family members.

EXERCISE #10—
STORYLINE DEVELOPMENT

Write a short story in a different genre than you have ever written in, a genre that you never thought you would write in. Challenge yourself to the max. If you normally write in third person, write in first person. If you normally write from a male perspective, write from a female perspective. If you usually write romance, write science fiction. If you normally write Christian fiction, write a story about vampires. If you usually write in past tense, write in present tense. The key is not to do anything that you normally do and see what develops. You may find that you actually like, or even prefer, one of the new techniques that you attempt.

These are ten exercises to get you started, but there are many books, websites, and blogs that can give you many more to choose from. You have to feed your brain like you feed your body. Writing should always be fun. Do not act like you are writing a term paper or that the world is on your shoulders. Do not get stressed out and allow worries to distract you from the bigger picture.

Another good idea is to join a local writers' group, or even get a writing partner. Set daily goals and make a commitment to email each other whatever you wrote at the end of the evening. Be accountable to each other and also give each other ideas. Remember that this should be about teamwork, not elimination. Just like people have exercise buddies that they walk or run with, or meet at the gym for a workout, you can have a writing exercise buddy as well.